Dead Men Do Tell Tales

60 Mini-Mysteries to Test Your Detective Prowess

Sherban Young

DOVER PUBLICATIONS, INC.
Mineola, New York

Bibliographical Note
Dead Men Do Tell Tales is a new work, first published by
Dover Publications, Inc., in 2010.

International Standard Book Number
ISBN-13: 978-0-486-47893-7
ISBN-10: 0-486-47893-9

Manufactured in the United States by Courier Corporation
47893901
www.doverpublications.com

Contents

Preface

Welcome to *Dead Men Do Tell Tales*. As you make your way through this trivia-themed mystery collection, poring over clues and identifying suspects, it's possible that the following question will cross your mind at some point:

How accurate are these things, really? Do murder investigations really work this way, and if they do, does this count as three questions or one?

All good thing(s) to know.

Personally, I'm all about the accuracy. I research. I consult. I even count correctly occasionally.

So it's probably not surprising, then, that in an effort to uphold this fine professional standard, I recently sat down with several leading experts in the field of criminal investigation and asked them about their work.

What they had to say shocked me.

According to the professionals, most crime scenes are not very well-organized. They don't tend to have a lot of obvious "clues" lying about, despite what Hollywood would have us believe. And they almost never, I am told, feature some variety of sleuth-friendly brainteaser designed to finger the guilty party.

You know the sort of thing I mean. A taunting scrap of poetry left behind by the whimsical and surprisingly well-read jewel thief. A crumpled violet clutched in the dead man's hand, referencing some telling secret from the past. The victim muttering "Why didn't they ask Evans?" with his last ounce of strength.

Doesn't happen, say these so-called experts. Nor does the investigation itself—and this I can hardly credit—usually turn up three handy suspects from which the willing amateur sleuth can select a perp.

I can draw but one conclusion from these expert claims, and one conclusion only. These leading experts have been pulling my leg. Unwilling to give away any trade secrets, and jealous of our stunning cerebral gifts, they have deliberately misled us, and for that they're more to be pitied than whatta-ya-call-it.

Nevertheless, whether elaborate puzzles figure into most murders or not, they do here. And they're almost always multiple choice. Picture the SATs, only more fun and with an extra corpse or two.

Dead Man Talking . . .

Now that we've gotten that squared away, let's discuss how to tackle these mystery puzzles. It's not always easy to know where to begin.

The crime game, after all, has changed. As modern sleuths, we can no longer rely on the tools of the past: the trusty magnifying glass, the fingerprint kit, the slide rule or whatever-it-was that determined the weight and density of cigar ash. As nifty as these things are—and they're pretty darn nifty—they won't help decipher any vital puzzle clues, now will they? Ask a fingerprint kit who composed "Carmina Burana," and it won't have any idea. Regarding the Battle of Hastings or the poet Tennyson, the magnifying glass is also notoriously silent.

No, in the world of scholarly murder mysteries, which this book specializes in, sometimes the only things standing between justice and a fictional killer laughing in his sleeve are the following:

1. **brains**
2. **a slide rule (optional)**
3. **the web**

I bet one item stands out from this list. That one thing all successful detectives must have in order to achieve their goals. Yes, you guessed it. The web. (A good, stout dictionary or other reference book will also do, but I prefer the net—it's the made-up murderer's worst enemy.)

I'll prove it to you. Let's say we stumble upon our dead body in the lobby of a hotel. In his hand we find a single clue—an old crumpled Babe Ruth baseball card. The victim is obviously trying to tell us something. From the gossipy bellhop we learn that the dead man recently had it out with three other guests: a woman named Beth Rogers (a ballroom dancer); a man registered as Bart Rollo (a noted card sharp); and some guy called George Herman (purveyor of stick-free spatulas).

At first glace, Beth Rogers might be our woman. She has the same initials as Babe Ruth. But so does Bart Rollo. Perhaps we'd better look to their professions. Beth is a ballroom dancer. Ballroom, baseball card. Interesting—but let's not forget that Bart is also a card sharp, and that could just as easily apply. Maybe we need a hint (included with every puzzle).

We turn to the hint page and read:

The answer's in the name

Curious. Let's do a search on Babe Ruth. Go online—or if the Internet isn't within reach, grab your favorite dictionary, and look up "Babe Ruth."

All right, lots of interesting things about Mr. Ruth. He played baseball. Good, good. He hit home runs. Yes, okay. But here's the really telling fact: he was born *George Herman Ruth*. We need look no further. Our spatula man has flipped his last tuna melt.

Now, many of you out there recognized the name George Herman at once and were slapping the cuffs on the poor man before he knew where he was. And if you think that makes you special—well okay, then.

They won't all be this easy.

Sherban Young

1.

Barroom Crawl

A man with a dagger in his back walked into a bar.

The bartender asked, "Whatta-ya have?"

The customer, who couldn't quite get out the words, reached over the counter and plucked an olive and a peel of lemon from the selection of garnishes. Presenting these to his host—first the olive then the lemon—he made a short gurgle and expired.

"Some loonies we get in here," muttered the bartender, and went back to polishing his glass.

The next day, the papers told of the local businessman slain the previous evening. Stabbed in the back, he had apparently fought his assailant off and somehow managed to stumble away and into a nearby tavern.

The suspects included three longtime associates.

First on the list was Charlotte Barnet, an opera singer from Madrid, on tour performing the title role in Bizet's *Carmen*.

Second there was Paul Jenkins, a Virginian bookstore owner, considered to be one of the industry's foremost experts on the works of Charles Dickens.

Lastly, the police were questioning Tom Riley, a used car salesman from California known for selling defective vehicles.

The bartender, reading the article, knew the murderer's identity immediately.

Who iced the bar guest?

Hint: Page 127
Solution: Page 136

1

2.
Trouble with the Help

The upstairs maid yanked the manor chef into the library. With a muffled gasp, she quivered from head to toe, pointed toward the desk, and said "Gurgum!"

The chef was in no mood for this. "What is it, Miss Agincourt? I got risotto burning on the stove, you know."

He was about to add something stinging about thoughtless chambermaids who pull good men away from their duties, when he finally spotted what she was so worked up about.

Across the library lay their employer, Colonel Milkweed, a well-known military historian. He was fatally run-through with an aborigine spear.

"Ah yes," remarked the chef, catching the gist, "one less for lunch today, gotcha."

Another curious gurgle escaped the maid. She was hopping up and down now and making odd little "eeping" noises.

"I've called the police, Mr. Jutland! When first I saw him, I called!"

"Good idea," agreed the chef, edging toward the door. "Now, if you don't mind . . ."

"But whoever could have killed him?"

"Couldn't tell you. We got no guests, so it must have been one of us. . . Do you know what happens when risotto burns, Miss Agincourt?"

"You mean one of us servants did it! Oh my! Oh dear! That just leaves, you . . . me . . . Mr. Bulge . . . Mr. Naseby . . . and Mrs. Hastings. Oh look!"

The chef looked.

"It's his pocket watch, Mr. Jutland. I saw it when I came in. Only, he must have diddled with it because it reads 4:45 and it's not even noon yet. He must have been trying to tell us something with it. Look, he's smashed it to stop it right there at that time."

The chef was done looking. "Kinda melodramatic, ain't it?" He thought people only did that sort of thing in mystery stories.

He took a step toward the door again, paused and glanced around at the array of history volumes. A wry smile played across his lips. "Ever wonder what the colonel meant when he said he only hired us servants because of our names?"

The maid gaped dully. She had often wondered that very thing.

"No matter how bad we were," the chef reflected, "and we're pretty bad, it's only the name that matters, he used to say."

"I've never understood that," the maid admitted.

"I think I just figured it out," said the chef. "And I also think I know who knocked off our employer."

Who jabbed the colonel?

Hint: Page 127
Solution: Page 136

3

3.
High Stakes Slaying

On the floor of the Vegas hotel room lay Vinnie Varoom, shot some fourteen times (several fatally).

"According to the scuttlebutt around the casino," one room-service waiter told another, standing over the corpse, "Vinnie borrowed ten grand from a local loan shark. The old story, he thought he could finish in the money at the Texas Hold'em tournament."

The other man nodded. He had seen it many times before. "Probably got it from one of the regular sources—Ricky Roads, Nick Nottingham or Teddy Thames. They're the common guys. Guess Vinnie didn't make it to the final table?"

"Guess not," his friend replied. He peered down at a row of playing cards, lined up along side the body. "Looks like Vinnie managed to deal out one last board."

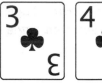

Vinnie's lifeless finger was pointing to the Ace.

"Think he was trying to tell us something?" the second waiter asked.

"I think he was," answered the first. "In fact, I think he was trying to tell us the murderer."

Who whacked Vinnie?

Hint: Page 127
Solution: Page 136

4

4.
Hollywood Hullabaloo

For the fifth time in as many minutes, the little old lady tried to push her way into the memorabilia shop. She wanted to buy some Hollywood collectibles and she wanted to buy them now.

The salesclerk held her at the door. "Sorry, ma'am, can't come in. Shop owner's been murdered."

The lady brightened. "Murdered? Must mean there's a sale? Is there a sale?"

"No sale," replied the clerk regretfully. "Murder. Can't come in."

"I like that lamp post," said the woman, pointing to a remnant from *Singing in the Rain* in the store window. "Sell me that lamp post."

"No lamp post," said the clerk. "Murder. Shop owner."

"Yes, yes, I heard you, young man. Who murdered him?"

"Dunno. One of his old actor chums, looks like. There were three of them in the shop at the time. Actually, you might remember them from the silver screen—these were the really ancient ones. Charlie Canning, made a career as the gruff sheriff; Tom Heywood, used to play military parts; and Arthur Wellesley, the quintessential gunslinger. The shop owner must've gotten into an argument with one of them, because there was some yelling, then the murderer must've picked up a brick from the set of *Mr. Blandings Builds His Dream House* and bonked my boss."

"I'll give you fifty bucks for the brick," offered the lady. "Provided you got a certificate of authenticity."

"It's funny," the clerk commented, leaning on the door frame. "The owner was found lying on an autographed photo of John Wayne. Looks like he made a grab for it just as the murderer was clobbering him. Funny, don't you think?"

The customer didn't. She already had an autographed Wayne. "If I tell you who bumped off your boss, can I come in?"

Who bumped him off?

Hint: Page 127
Solution: Page 137

5.
Death of Art

The temperamental artist made a sweeping, petulant gesture.

"I cannot work this way!" he exclaimed, indicating with another mighty flourish the musty bookshop all around him.

His agent appeared at his side, a look of kindly concern on her face. "Problem, Raoul?"

The artist snorted magnificently. "You ask me if there is a problem? I say yes problem, very much one. I am here for the autograph session, yes? Signing of my book *Raoul: Portrait of a Genius*, correct? But what pains do I get? Many! The girl, she is late with the coffee, and when it comes, it is not to my loving. The customers, they do not know me! They say, who is this, and do not know it is the great Raoul!"

The agent smoothed her client's rumpled jerkin. "I'm sorry, Raoul. They're philistines, all of them. It'll be better after lunch, honest."

"And that is not it!" said the artist, pointing. "This body, I no like! Raoul goes to find better coffee and there is this! A body dead, near his podium! It does nothing either, just lies there, mockingly! What is this, then?"

For the first time in the conversation the agent noticed the corpse in the Fine Arts section. He was lying face up with a large nail file protruding from his Adam's apple.

Closer scrutiny revealed that he was also gripping a book on the work of the Flemish painter Rubens—not the masterpiece that was *Raoul: Portrait of a Genius*, but a very fine text.

"Oh my!" exclaimed the agent, and went off to find the store manager.

"They're calling the police," she told her client a few minutes later, to which Raoul wondered how this addressed the essential issue at hand, i.e. Raoul. "Apparently the dead man is one of the employees here. You won't believe this, Raoul, but his name is Art."

"Pah!"

"Strictly between you and me, he was having a dalliance with one of the young ladies he worked with, no one knows who, and they think there must have been an altercation, and she jabbed him with that large nail file."

"A very sloppy murder," said Raoul. "No panache, no flair. I give it none of my consideration."

"They all seemed like such nice girls too," continued the agent. "I mean, little Veranda, who helped us set up—"

"A mousy young thing. Small, with tiny hips. I could not paint her."

"Or Florence, the assistant manager! She was so kind on the phone!"

"The buxom blonde," spoke Raoul wistfully. "I lose myself in her ample curves. Yes, she is nice. Raoul likes."

"Or Genevieve! I can't see her doing this either, can you?"

"She bring me no coffee, this Genevieve," muttered the temperamental artist. "She is very statuesque, that girl. The skinny amazon with the long hair. I would paint her, yes, but with a canvas very tall. This tall," he indicated.

"I don't see how any of these nice girls could have done it."

The artist shook his head. "Ah, but it is too obvious, is it not? It is not worthy of my talents."

And on that sentiment, he went off to find himself that coffee.

Who defaced Art?

Hint: Page 127
Solution: Page 137

8

6.
Classic Bravado

The minute Harry tripped the silent alarm, the guards were after him. They chased him up the road, around the corner and down a backstreet. He had just managed to hurry into a hotel before they closed in on him.

Baffled by the perp's footwork in the lobby, they lost him momentarily in the stairwell, eventually tracking him down to Room 83, thanks to a tip from a somewhat languid bellhop (who sadly did not receive a tip in return).

Kicking in the door, they found Harry sitting in a chair with his feet up. He was smoking a cigarette, content in the knowledge that the patented cure for baldness he had just stolen was safe and his partner Sidney would know exactly where he had hidden it—that is, once Sid saw his clue.

The clue in question would appear to be the words "FJH's surprise" written on a scrap of paper and taped to the radio.

"He must have hidden the goo in some other room," said the guard, after a cursory search of the modest surroundings.

"But which one?" wondered his buddy. "And what if somebody finds the stuff before we do?" He kicked the mini bar, which hadn't been refilled in months.

"I think I can help, gentlemen," said the hotel manager, looking in from the splintered doorframe. He lent an air of class to the otherwise classless surroundings. "The note on the radio is quite specific about where we might find the missing formula. If you'll follow me, I will take you there. Only, if you do not mind, we'll use the passkey this time. We're but a humble hotel, and we need our doors."

Where'd Harry stash the goo?

Hint: Page 127
Solution: Page 137

9

7.
Nod if You Know It

The smug and opinionated baseball journalist lay facedown in the pâté, poisoned. The rest of the team reunion had gone off without a hitch, and some would say the murder was the highlight of a delightful evening.

Two retired umpires had discovered the body in the back of the banquet hall.

"It's a murder, that's what it is. One of the sponsors from the business community obviously did him in. My money's on the feller who sat der. The file drawer manufacturer."

The umpire behind the plate—the pâté plate—disagreed.

"You're crazy, buddy. I was watching the whole time, and the killer was the mapmaker, no question. Fast hands that guy had. He could poison a plate of pâté as soon as look atcha. That's the answer. Or maybe it was the calendar printer. That could be it. But not the file drawer guy, nuh uh."

"Now, listen, don't be arguing with me," said his buddy.

"Don't be arguing with *me*," said his chum.

"You gonna make an issue outta this?"

"Are *you*?"

"Whoa there, guys, take it easy," said a third umpire, joining the fray. "Now then, what's all the hubbub about? And before you answer that, what's up with all the bobbleheads?"

Indeed, in front of the dead reporter sat three cheerful bobblehead dolls in a row, depictions of some ex-players who had been invited to the event that day: an ex-first baseman, an ex-shortstop and an ex-third baseman.

Evidently the journalist, realizing which one of the sponsors had poisoned him, had just enough time to arrange the bobbles in this particular order before succumbing to his fate.

"Oh, if that's what it is," said the third umpire knowingly, "then it's obvious whodunit."

"Not obvious to me," said the first umpire.

"Me neither," said the second, glaring.

"Well, I'm outta here, then!" replied the third, and went off to report his findings to the police.

Who pitched the poisoned pâté?

Hint: Page 127
Solution: Page 138

8.
Food for Thought

The eminent restaurant critic, J. B. Sniffwell, announced his presence in the kitchen with a haughty snort.

"Since you asked me back here," he told the bistro owner, "I might as well tell you what I thought of my luncheon. I found the shrimp stringy, the bisque gluey and the arugula below par. And," he remarked, for he was a man who pulled no punches, "I don't much like the look of that corpse there with the meat cleaver in its back."

It was the matter of the corpse—sprawled out on the kitchen tile courtesy of the aforementioned meat cleaver—that was concerning the owner.

"J. B.! Someone has murdered my French chef Pierre!"

Sniffwell replied that it was not he; although his tone suggested that he would have had every right to do so, considering the quality of his meal. He gazed down through lazy eyelids at a solitary tomato, squished in the cook's right hand.

"Hothouse," he commented dryly.

"The police are taking forever!" uttered the owner. "I thought you might have seen who did it. It has to be one of those women in the dining room; they're the only ones here."

"Well, I certainly did not keep tabs on who came and went," replied Sniffwell. "I was too occupied sampling the salmon mousse—which lacked true substance, I might add."

"It has to be one of these women," continued the owner, unconcerned with insubstantial mousse. "You'll hardly credit this, but they were his girlfriends, all three of them. They must have gotten wise to his affairs, because one of them obviously came back here and killed him."

"Seems reasonable," said Sniffwell. It was unclear whether he meant the supposition or the murder.

"Freya Pippin, Vesta Frappe and Paisley Grace. Those are the girls, and one of them did it—I'm sure of it. You certain you didn't see which one got up from her table?"

"I am certain," Sniffwell agreed. He peered back at the tomato, and smiled. "It is evident, however, that your cook did see the murderess, because he left us a valuable clue. It's fortunate that you have me here to decipher it," he concluded modestly.

Who carved the French chef?

Hint: Page 128
Solution: Page 138

9.
Billiard Blues

Backstage in the tournament dressing rooms, two television commentators inspected the body of the murdered billiard finalist.

"Well, Chet, looks like Pete Pastel is out of the tourney permanently. Sam Schwarz, Victor Verdi and Baxter Blanco are gonna have to fight this one out themselves in the final round."

"That they will, Tom. Pete's been eliminated, no question. Electrocuted, unless I miss my guess."

"Electrocuted it is. Apparently someone snuck in and tossed this hair dryer into his foot bath when he wasn't looking. One of the oldest tricks around. Of course, in billiards, you always have to watch out for trick *shocks*, don't you, Chet?"

"Ho-ho, don't get me started. Now, this is funny. Standing over the corpse I see Pete has managed to rip out two pages from the new contestant welcome manual: pages six and fourteen. He's laid them out for us."

"That he has, Chet—614. That's how old you were last birthday, wasn't it?"

"Har-har, you don't know the half of it. Seriously, though. I bet he was trying to name the killer with these. Hey now, I think I see what Pete was driving at."

"Do you? Well, I always figured you'd have a thought one of these days."

"Ho-ho, don't get me started."

Who racked up Pete?

Hint: Page 128
Solution: Page 139

10.
Tundra Turnover

In the far reaches of the frozen tundra, the body of expert explorer Sir Percival Flick lay atop the barren earth, shot in the back with his own revolver. His two partners, Ned Winslow and Max Cooper, gathered around him. They appeared concerned.

"This is not good," said Max.

"No, I know," replied Ned. "Percy was the only one who knew how to use the compass." He retrieved the item in question from the dead man's hand and studied it. "Think we're supposed to go that-a-way?" he asked.

Max shrugged. With a sigh, he contemplated the stiff explorer at his feet, made stiffer still by the harsh artic winds. In Percy's other hand were seven bullets from his ammo belt, all .45 caliber. Max picked these up.

"What he wanted to do, of course, was put these in a gun and fire them at his murderer."

"That would've done the trick, all right," Ned agreed. "Still, I think he was trying to tell us something. Relay a message of some sort, don't you think?"

"Like the identity of the killer? Man, it's nippy out here!"

"Yes, something like that." A curious look came over Ned Winslow's face. He looked from the bullets to the compass and then back to the bullets again. "Oh, I see what Flick was getting at now."

Well, what was he?

Hint: Page 128
Solution: Page 139

15

11.
A Nut at Every Party

The time was getting on to six a.m., and the party at Centerfold Mansion was just beginning to wind down. About half the guest list had already wandered home, when one of the stragglers stumbled over to the bar and swatted Miss October on the behind.

"Hiya, honey buns! How's about getting me a gin'n'tonic."

"I am not a waitress," said the young lady, grasping the inebriate's hand in a compelling judo grip. Aside from martial arts, her hobbies included skiing and purchasing negligees.

"How 'bout you two?" he asked, trying to focus in on Miss August and Miss February. "There *are* two of ya there, right?"

"Why don't we call you a cab, friend," said the second one, nodding.

The guest smiled. "Sure thing, honey bun, or should I say *buns-es*. But before I go, lemme get a couple of drinks for my friends over there. That'll be two gin'n'tonics, a gimlet, a whisky sour no ice, a martini no olive, an olive no martini, and, oh, a dead guy on the veranda."

Miss August, listening intently, had never heard of the last selection. "Is that made straight up or on the rocks?" she wondered prettily. An avid polo player and performer of interpretive dance, she always liked to learn new things.

The guy blinked. "No, I mean there's an actual dead guy out there. The olive's for 'im."

The three centerfolds glanced between themselves, and the guest continued, "Reed Busby, the photographer. That's who it looks like. We'd been seeing him with waitress babes all night—Rachael, Roxanne, Barbara—all the babes. Me and my friends looked 'im over, and it seems to us he was poisoned, in that someone must have poisoned 'im. Probably one of those babes. Hey, did I say we need a gin'n'tonic? Good, 'cause we do. Of course, the funny thing is that row of nuts. On the table near where we found 'im, there's this row of nuts, in that I mean nuts, all in a row. And very particular nuts they are too. Can't remember the last time I saw more particular nuts. Like they mean something or something. Pecan, macadamia, cashew, pecan, macadamia, cashew—keeps repeating pecan, macadamia, cashew. Wait, I'll show ya."

"That's the row of nuts," he concluded. "Looks like he messed it up at the end, though. The extra macadamia. That's why I say never try and arrange nuts after you've been poisoned."

Miss February frowned. "Are you familiar with cryptograms, fella?"

"That made with tequila?"

"No, *honey bun,* a murder."

"Better add some tequila," inserted Miss August thoughtfully.

Who killed Busby?

Hint: Page 128
Solution: Page 139

12.
Help with the Trouble

The butler appeared gracefully on the threshold of his employer's botanical garden. The time was precisely 9:29 in the evening.

"Your bug squirter, Sir Martin, sir," he announced in a measured voice, carefully placing the salver containing the object on a nearby side table. "If there is nothing else, sir?"

A brief stage wait. The butler bowed slightly at the waist.

"Very good, sir. I can see you have been murdered. Most distressing," he added, for he could loosen up when the moment called for it.

Still addressing his employer's corpse, currently pinned to the back wall by a pair of pruning sheers, he said, "If you will excuse me, sir, I will now phone the authorities."

He turned to leave, pausing momentarily as a curious sound met his ears. This curious sound was silence.

Sir Martin Dingle, besides being an expert horticulturist, was also an incredible stickler for the correct time. All the clocks in his mansion were maintained with a compulsive precision, and all his servants were taught to respect and uphold this compulsion.

It therefore struck the butler as odd that the clock hanging within arm's reach of his late employer should have failed to chime.

He examined the clock and found the solution. The pendulum lay still—someone had evidently disabled it. What is more, someone had also set the time to four-o'clock— perhaps the same person, although the butler did not wish to overstep his bounds with idle speculation.

It was odd, however.

As usual, Sir Martin had entertained three guests at dinner tonight, all from the horticultural society. First there was the Duke of Barnaby, Sir Martin's loud and opinionated uncle—even louder and more opinionated than Sir Martin himself. He was full of descriptions of a flower show he had just attended in the south of France.

Next came Juan Mungo, a businessman from Peru, in town to give a lecture on water absorption in perennials.

Finally, they had Jane Biddle, head of the Hanover branch of the society and bitter rival of Sir Martin's. There had been bad feelings there ever since the two had fallen into discord over the use of posies at the club's last function.

One of them had to be the killer. The inaccurate four-o'clock, mostly likely set by Sir Martin himself, must have been arranged that way in order to identify that very person.

"Ah yes," said the butler, now cognizant of the solution. "I see. Very good, sir."

He glided from the room.

Who dingled Dingle?

Hint: Page 128
Solution: Page 140

13.
Out with the Clue

A light flicked on in the office of Otto's Discount Outerwear, illuminating the nocturnal activities of that well-known and devoted criminal couple, Duke and Deidre.

Deidre had begun rifling the desk, while Duke, a man who believed in giving his spouse her space, stood off to the side, idly browsing through loose merchandise. He had just picked up a pair of galoshes when she spoke.

"Like I said, honey, if Otto wanted to leave a clue about the loot, something the cops wouldn't recognize when they nabbed him, it would be here. And whatta-ya know, here's something now." She paused and read. "Take a gander at this."

**Seneca would have to travel
far to drink a little Hemlock**

Her hubby finished reading, pacing the office thoughtfully. "Do you like these galoshes?" he asked.

A travel umbrella sailed across the room, nearly clipping him in the noggin.

"We got work to do, darling," said his wife.

"Yes, darling."

"This is no time for shopping."

"Nope."

"So whatta-ya think this clue means?"

"Dunno."

The brains of the couple took a deep breath. "Well, think, puddin', think!" she said. An impassioned request, but perhaps one beyond the scope of her Duke. He selected a coonskin cap and placed it on his head, assuming a vague model's pose as he did so.

Deidre sat on the edge of the desk and frowned. "Okay—let's review. We're agreed that Otto's counterfeiting equipment can't be stashed anywhere around here, right? He must have hidden it at one of his factories. But which one? He's got so many. I mean, he's got a factory for footwear in Florida—"

"Galoshes," said Duke, only to be waved down by the love of his life.

"And a factory for headwear in Maine," she went on.

Duke tipped his coonskin.

"And a factory for gloves in New York."

Duke wondered if they had cashmere.

"The list goes on and on," she said.

"I look good in pelt," smiled her husband, gazing in the mirror.

"I mean, what could this gibberish mean! Seneca didn't drink hemlock, that was that other fella—Aristotle. I tell you, pumpkin, if Otto ever gets out of the pen I'm gonna stick this clue— Whoa, hold on. Darling, I think I'm onto something here!"

"Oo, look, earmuffs!" said Duke.

Where'd Otto stick the stuff?

Hint: Page 128
Solution: Page 140

14.
In Line with Flick

With one last powerful thrust, "Dashing" Dan Paddington-Paddington-Phipps, O.B.E., pulled himself up onto the cliff's edge, scattering pebbles into the darkened jungle below.

"We've made it, Jensen!" he shouted, addressing his faithful sidekick.

"Huh?" came a voice from the foot of the crag.

"I said we've made it. We've found the tomb of the ancient race of the Kweeby-Jeebie!"

"Good-o. Let me know when we got the treasure."

Dashing Dan approached the entrance of the tomb with that very aim in mind. A noted archeologist, part-time Oxford literature professor and occasional treasure hunter (when scheduling demands allowed), he was well-versed in all aspects of the ancient Kweeby. He knew from past experience that they were brilliant trap-makers. Not far from here, one of Dan's hapless guides, failing to observe the appropriate sequence into a Jeebie monument, had found himself riddled with spears, chased by a gigantic tarantula, and eventually plunged into a pit of deadly adders.

A most painful experience, to be sure.

Dashing Dan knew better than to let himself in for that. He also knew that the greatest of all explorers (not counting himself) had already done what he sought to do. Sir Percival Flick, tragically murdered in the frozen tundra a month before, had successfully navigated these very tunnels prior to his unfortunate end. Disinterested in monetary gain, he had allegedly left the treasure intact. All of which worked for Dan.

"I'm going in," he announced.

"What about my sister Gwen?" yelled Jensen.

Dan paid him no heed. He walked forward into the cave, at which point his head collided with something solid and he said, "Ooch."

Evidently it wasn't a cave at all, but rather a cleverly painted cave depiction—a common deception of the time and one that never failed to amuse the ancients.

"I say, it's a fake! There must be another entrance. Hallo, what's this? There's a clue carved here, from Sir Percival. Listen to this, Jensen—

> 'If you are reading this, Paddington, all I can say is well done, old friend, you have nearly unearthed the tomb of the Kweeby-Jeebie (which I have already done, but hey.) At any rate, the treasure awaits you, but before I can tell you how to get around this painted artifice, I must first explain that I have observed a band of greedy louts on my trail, members of Sir Martin Dingle's party, hoping to plunder the treasure we seek to preserve. And while I know you are something of a lout yourself, at least you're not a greedy lout. Therefore, to ensure that the right sort finds the goods, I have left behind a series of clues designed to illuminate matters for you but not for them (find the first below). Good Luck!
>
> —Sir Percival Flick.
>
> P.S.—You still owe me sixteen pounds four pence for last year's supper of the Manchester Explorers. Try to have the correct change when we meet.' "

Dashing Dan stepped back from the message. "Did you get all that, Jensen?"

"Get what?"

"Never mind. Here's the clue. Let's give it a go, what?"

"Goat? What goat? This is the first I've heard of any goats!"

"Here's the clue," stated Dan firmly.

**Down below at the foot of this crest, find you a
series of three panels, which will help you in your
quest. Three beautiful maidens they do depict:
Aletheia, Dione, Phoebe are their names, but
please restrict—pressing one will open doors, the
other two adversely score. A grisly death you can
avoid, but don't screw up or you'll be annoyed.
From the poet's immortal words the road to beauty
flows—and "This is all ye know on earth, and all
ye need to know."
That is the only clue I can offer here. Now push
on, my not-quite-peer.**

Dan leaned out over the ravine. "Make any sense?"

The echoing "Did what make any sense?" indicated that
it did not.

The dashing explorer strolled the cliff ledge, rubbing that
chiseled Paddington-Paddington jaw. "Well, I can't make heads
or tails of it. Do you see the three panels, the ones depicting
Aletheia, Dione and Phoebe?"

"Yeah. They're hot."

"Splendid. Well, you'll just have to push them all, I guess.
Even if it means getting thrown to the adders or chewed by
giant tarantulas, we must try, what?"

Jensen made no reply.

"I say, Jensen? Are you there? I said we must try?"

"Not on," answered the Jensen echo aloofly.

Dan peered out over the rock face. "My dear fellow,
where's your backbone? You have a one-in-three chance of
success here. Those are stats any decent baseball player
would snap up in a minute."

"Not cricket," said Jensen.

Dan frowned. "Well, I'm disappointed in you, Jensen. Think
of the gold, the emeralds. The diamonds and whatnot."

"Can't buy you love," argued his sidekick.

Dashing Dan shook his head. "I'm not saying *you will*
be chewed by tarantulas, Jensen, only that you *might be*

chewed. Now stiffen the upper lip and go to it. Do the name of Jensen proud! Step up, press one of those beauties and . . . " Dan paused. "Hold on, I think I've got it. The answer to the clue!"

"Well, go to it, then," Jensen remarked. "I'll follow once you've made the name Paddington-Paddington proud."

Which panel opens the secret entrance?

Hint: Page 129
Solution: Page 140

15.
Barroom Sprawl

A man with a grill fork in his back stumbled into a bar.

The bartender asked, "What can I get ya, pal?"

The customer, who didn't feel much like talking, staggered over to the counter, selecting a fifth of vodka and a carton of orange juice. With an effort, he slid these toward the other man, burbled slightly and keeled over dead.

"Hey, buddy, we just cleaned these floors," said the bartender, refilling the peanut bowls.

Later that evening, the cops came to collect the body. They explained that the murdered man, a real Lothario, had evidently been set upon by a jealous husband at a neighborhood picnic.

The police had pulled in three suspects for questioning: Tom Dryden, a grocery store manager, whose wife Cynthia had recently spent the weekend with the dead man at the national pomegranate festival; Boris Glinka, an orchestra conductor, whose wife Colleen was once found giving the murdered man an oboe lesson in the nude; and finally Jake Preston, a hardware store owner, whose wife Guinevere used to personally bring the victim his order for lug nuts at Naughty Nanette's Erotic Motel & Massage.

One of these three men was believed to have forked the neighborhood Don Juan when no one was looking.

Offering the officers a peanut, the bartender explained who did it.

Who punctured the playboy?

Hint: Page 129
Solution: Page 140

26

16.
Hang on

The impressive figure of Mr. Crocker, owner of the impressive telemarketing agency Crocker Ltd., loomed up at the cubical of one of his less than impressive junior telemarketers, Harold Bentley.

"Bentley!" he vociferated. "The Mundlebee quota, Bentley! How many Mundlebee kits have you sold today, because it's not enough! Get me your Mundlebee totals!"

Bentley, slumped across his desk, made no attempt to comply with this simple request. This might have had something to do with the telephone cord wrapped around his throat, but it was difficult to tell for sure. He was holding the phone's handset in his right hand; and it was the handset that now chimed in with a breezy, though slightly irrelevant, "If you would like to make a call please hang up and . . ."

This was of no value to Mr. Crocker. "Are you listening to me, Bentley! I don't have time for this drivel! I've already had to deal with dipping numbers from your co-workers, and I've had enough, you hear me, enough! Aldrich hasn't sold any countertops this week; Beckett is a washout on magazine subscriptions; and Collins is way behind on trips to Costa Rica. And now I suppose one of them has strangled you with your own telephone cord! Harrumph! You four always were competing over the *glamorous* customer lists, and now it's come to this, has it? Well, this will not reflect favorably on your salary review, Bentley, not favorably at all! Crocker Ltd. does not look kindly on employees who get themselves murdered on company time! Well, what do you have to say for yourself!"

The Bentley corpse had nothing to say for itself. Few corpses ever did after one of Mr. Crocker's magnificent harangues. The handset, meanwhile, was still inserting its two cents.

"The number you have called—265-5467—cannot be completed as dialed. If you would like to make a call, please . . . "

Mr. Crocker snorted. He had identified the murderer but he didn't see how that would get him his Mundlebee totals.

Who hung up on Bentley?

Hint: Page 129
Solution: Page 141

17.
A Note of Violence

The stock boy at Ernie's Record Emporium stepped out of the back office and ran a hand through his greasy hair. Drawing comfort from this small gesture, he took a deep breath and said, "No one go anywhere, okay. Ernie's been, like, murdered."

The store's three customers exchanged a questioning glance across the aisles.

The stock boy continued, "It must have just happened, because I was, like, in the back not two minutes ago, and Ernie was there shrink-wrapping some albums with this shrink-wrap thing we have—it's this sort of thing we have for, like, shrink-wrapping. Anyway, he was like 'I thought I fired you' and I was like 'No, man, not this week' and he was like 'Well, get me a pack of cigarettes then' and I was like 'Whatever, dude.' And what I'm trying to point out is, he was completely alive when he said this. The thing is, I went back a second later and he's like totally dead now. Shrink-wrapped to death. Not pretty. That's when I was like 'Whoa! Not cool!' and came out here. And what I'm trying to emphasize is I think Ernie, like, recognized his killer and left us a clue about this very uncool party."

The patrons shared another bewildered stare.

"Actually, the clue is playing right now," said the clerk. "'52nd Street Theme' by that Charlie Parker guy. It wasn't playing when I was back there the first time and it wasn't due up in the changer for another half-hour. Ernie must have picked it on purpose. I theorize the killer came back to Ernie's office to kill him—the dude had enough enemies—

and Ernie somehow managed to put this song playing before the killer did the killing. And now all we have to do is, like, figure out who it was. In order to complete my investigation, I will need to ask you all some questions."

The audience began to rankle at the suggestion. The stock boy paid them no attention.

"Okay, you—dude in the back—what's your story?"

The dude in the back's story was that he was Bob White, a banker from Rhode Island.

This struck the stock boy as significant. "*Rhode* Island, eh. Sounds an awful lot like *road* to me, man. Road. Street. 52nd Street. I gotta tell you, banker dude, it isn't looking good for you, not good at all. Okay, what about you, tan babe?"

The tan babe, as she very much resented being called, was Elizabeth Green, a wealthy socialite visiting from the Island of Rhodes in Greece.

This seemed to disappoint the clerk. "Isle of *Rhodes*, huh. You're not helping, Greek chick. Okay, what about you, third guy?"

The third guy was Riley Brown, a student. Originally from New Haven, Riley had recently spent some time studying in England.

This perked up the stockroom detective considerably. Any good makeshift PI jumps at the chance to pare down his list, and there was clearly no connection between streets or roads and the life of Riley.

"Cool, man. New Haven and England. Nothing road-y about that. Where in England?"

Oxford. Riley had gone there as a Rhodes scholar.

The stock boy mulled this over. In the background, Charlie Parker and the gang had moved onto the next track, "Just Friends," a sentiment not reflected in the store at the moment.

"Well, I guess we'll have to leave it to the cops," said the stock boy resignedly. "I mean, I don't pretend to be Miss

Marple or anything, and if you all are gonna insist on having 'road' sounding words— Oh, whoa, an idea just zoomed in there. Man, I nearly let that one get away!"

Who eliminated Ernie?

Hint: Page 129
Solution: Page 141

18
A Foodie Cooked

The eminent restaurant critic, J. B. Sniffwell, that magnificent exponent of good taste, leaned back in his chair with a frown. His soup, a creamy butternut squash, had not been the unspeakable rubbish he predicted it would be. This boded well for the main course, which might not turn out to be utter crapola.

Sufficiently mellowed, he took another sip of wine—an inferior vintage but not without its charm—and was in the process of examining its color in the light when a nervous waitress appeared at his side. She seemed more agitated than usual.

"There's a problem with your lunch, Mr. Sniffwell!"

"My dear young lady," said the restaurant critic, speaking in a tolerant drawl, "when it comes to problems I hardly think you can match my previous visit. In case you've forgotten, it featured a grisly murder in the kitchen. Now then, what is the nature of our crisis today?"

"There's been a grisly murder in the kitchen!"

Sniffwell nodded calmly. "I see. The chef again?"

"No, the owner. But the chef freaked out, and knocked over a tray of grilled salmon."

"I don't blame him. I have tasted his béarnaise."

"So we got a dead owner and a freaked-out chef," concluded the waitress.

"I was told there were no specials," quipped Sniffwell.

"And someone in this restaurant right now is a murderer!"

"There are worse things in life, young lady. This rémoulade for instance."

She leaned in closer—J. B. often had this effect on women. "I think one of the ensemble did it," she whispered, jerking a surreptitious thumb toward the trio of musicians at the front of the room. Dressed in period garb, they were performing a pleasant medieval melody.

Sniffwell took a measured glance at the threesome. "And what in particular has cast suspicion on these three poor troubadours?"

"Well, they're always in and out of the kitchen, and just this morning all three of them had it out with the boss about their salary. Evidently they wanted one. And when we found the boss's body in the back near the freezer, he was gripping an advertisement from the ensemble in one hand and a postcard from Boston in the other. He must have grabbed it during the murder. Whichever one did him in used a frozen leg of lamb."

"I have not tried the lamb," observed Sniffwell thoughtfully. "Are any of these musicians from Massachusetts?" he wondered.

The waitress shook her head.

"Well then, I have nothing to offer. Don't get me wrong, this has been most diverting, but I do not see how a postcard from Boston could relate to a flutist, a lute player or a cellist. Perhaps that gentlemen in the back asking for a refill on his iced tea wishes to share a theory."

The waitress left to attend to her pesky customer, and for a moment nothing could be heard save the sound of wine trickling into a glass and a trio of poor troubadours.

"My dear Sniffwell," spoke a light, mocking voice then, "you really are a most astounding halfwit."

Sniffwell turned slowly in his chair, appalled to discover the obnoxious figure of J. D. Tinkery, the contemptible music critic for the *Gazette*, sitting at the next table.

"Oh, it's you, J. D."

"It is I," Tinkery agreed. "I've been listening to you spout away for the past ten minutes, and I must say I am astonished, utterly astonished. You might know food, J. B., but when it comes to music, you haven't a notion."

"In what manner do I fall short of the ideal?"

"Talking about these musicians, for one thing. You got it all wrong."

"They aren't musicians?"

"Oh, they're musicians, all right. I'm here to review them, in fact. But they're using *period* instruments. Not all from the same period, mind you, but one smiles at the effort. The instrument you casually referred to as a flute, is in actuality a flageolet. What you call a cello is more precisely a viol, and the lute—really, J. B., I'm surprised at you—the lute is a mandolin."

"I stand corrected," replied Sniffwell, finishing his claret. "I suppose, now that one of the trio is about to be arrested, you'll be leaving. A pity."

"Arrested? On what basis? Certainly nothing you had to offer. Har-har!"

"On the contrary," Sniffwell remarked. "Thanks to your gracious footnotes I now know the identity of the killer and am prepared to expose him. Play that on your crumhorn sometime."

Who clobbered the restaurateur?

Hint: Page 129
Solution: Page 141

19.
Letter of the Law

Ozzie Windell, partner in the law firm of Fibs, Windell, Hooley, Gann and Hood, had been gunned down in his lavish office. They found him sprawled out on the carpet, next to a row of lettered game tiles.

A couple of legal clerks had indulged Oz in a game earlier that evening, eventually leaving due to other commitments. When they left, he was saying something about the loss of valuable points, having been saddled with so many Q's, X's and Z's, and had even declared that he had a good mind to file a class action suit against the makers of the game.

One of these clerks had discovered the body later that evening and brought in Misters Hooley, Gann and Hood for consultation. Mr. Fibs, currently engaged in over-billing a client, would join the deliberation on his way back from Accounting.

"Clearly murder one," announced Mr. Gann, small and weasely in appearance.

Mr. Hooley, smaller and more weasely, nodded, whispering something about *prima facie.*

"Perhaps one of his clients did it," commented Mr. Hood languidly.

Mr. Hooley, still weasely, muttered something about *jurisprudence.*

"Wonder if this qualifies for workman's comp," contributed the arriving Mr. Fibs, who in addition to being short and weasely, was also wizened and sneering.

Mr. Hooley grumbled something about *ex gratia.*

"I mean, any number of his clients' ex-wives wanted to do him in," continued Fibs. "They all hated him. It could have been Chloe, the ex-Mrs. Madison. She always had a hot temper. Then there's Candy, the ex-Mrs. Peterson, what a firecracker. And let's not forget Cindy, the ex-Mrs. Gunther—whoa, boy, that lady was—"

"Yes, yes, never mind all that," objected Mr. Gann. "Look at these tiles." He pointed at the game tiles laid out on the carpet. No doubt placed there by Oz himself, they appeared to form a short sentence. It was difficult to tell this for sure, however, for Oz's legal pad was cutting off the bottom half of the tiles.

Mr. Gann, suggesting his partners look the other way, kicked the pad aside. (Mr. Hooley, well-versed in tampering with evidence, said something about *in situ* and *in medias res*, and then added something else no one caught about *in vino veritas.)*

The tiles were unveiled.

G U I Q F   S U Q T   Q Z

"Is G-U-I-Q-F a word?" wondered Mr. Hood, perusing the uncovered sentence.

"I haven't come across it in any law reviews," said Mr. Gann.

"I think the old boy was sloshed," clucked Mr. Fibs.

"Clearly sauced," seconded Mr. Gann.

"I don't think he was," said a voice.

Tall, elegant and not particularly weasely—clearly nothing more than a lowly associate—the newcomer had been listening to his superiors' comments with interest.

He was now prepared to give them his own version of the facts. "If it pleases the gathering, I can tell you who killed Mr. Windell, and then perhaps we can talk about who makes partner in Oz's place."

Who knocked off Oz?

Hint: Page 129
Solution: Page 142

20.
Slaying in Hand

The manager of the hotel found two of his room service waiters lounging idly in the hall. Contrary to popular opinion, this was not what he was paying them for.

"I tell you, it's fair," one was saying to the other. "Money well-deserved."

"And I tell you it ain't right," the other was arguing. "Ain't right at all."

"What compelling issue are we discussing here, gentlemen?" interrupted the manager. "Your salary reviews, or the big hand that won yesterday's Texas Hold'em tournament?"

"Neither," responded the employee on the right. "Although that was some bad beat, wasn't it? Seven-five taking down pocket aces."

"Major bad beat," concurred his cohort. "Actually, boss, we were discussing whether we should charge the guy who won the tourney a corkage fee. We were just in his room, and he's got a bottle of champagne in there, not one of ours."

"And what does Mr. Cashman have to say for himself?"

"Nuthin', boss."

"He's dead," explained the first waiter. "Poisoned by the champagne. It looks like one of his opponents did him in. After winning the tourney last night he went celebrating with the three guys he beat at the final table. Never a good idea. I watched them film these guys earlier, and the guy he beat heads-up was a fella named Flunkerton, used to be a college professor in the Bayou State. That's the guy Cashman beat with seven-five. The guy he took down when it was three-handed was named Welderstein, just sold his body shop in Motor City. Welderstein got his pocket jacks beat by Cashman's ten-seven—suited, but still ten-seven. The guy he snookered four-handed was some stage actor bozo, Leadingham I think his name was, recently cut from *Phantom of the Opera* on the Great White Way. Poor guy had his Kings cracked by Cashman's queen-six. Queen-six!"

"And these three shared the champagne with Mr. Cashman?"

"Yeah, and one of them must've poisoned the bottle. Could have been any of them. Cashman sucked out on everybody."

"Indeed. Have you phoned the police?"

"Not until we decide what to do about the corkage, boss."

"And there's still the matter of our tip," said the other man. "By the way, when the cops get here, you can give them these cards. They were in Cashman's hand. It's remotely possible that he reached for these in order to, I don't know, tell us something."

The manager nodded pensively. A poker player himself, like everyone else who worked in the Vegas hotel, it was clear to him who committed the murder now. It was also clear that he needed to hire more competent waiters. One thing at a time, however.

Whose bitterness spilled over to murder?

Hint: Page 129
Solution: Page 142

21.
Shakespeare Shenanigans

The campus security guard burst into the English Lit classroom.

There, slumped on the floor between the chalkboard and a pair of frat boys arguing over who partied harder—Rosencrantz or Guildenstern—lay the poor murdered college professor, bludgeoned to death with his own antique typewriter.

In the back stood the three suspects, neatly arranged there by the teacher's pet, who claimed to know jujitsu. All three were troublemakers, and each had been scheduled to meet with the professor that day to rehearse "Great Murderers from Shakespeare," a class presentation.

One was to play Brutus from *Julius Caesar*, another King Claudius from *Hamlet*, and the last was to play Macbeth from—you guessed it—*Macbeth*.

"Guess someone took his role a little too seriously," the guard sighed, glancing down at the body. "Hey now, what's this?" He alluded to an assortment of typewriter keys, scattered across the floor.

One of the frat boys speculated that they had come loose from the typewriter during the bludgeoning. This theory sounded plausible to the guard, who had been a Sigma Chi.

The "t," "2" and "e" were found in the grasp of the professor.

"He must have been trying to name the killer," said the guard. "But what could a '2,' a 't' and an 'e' mean?"

"Oo! oo! I know," squawked the teacher's pet. The kiss up.

Who bonked the professor?

Hint: Page 130
Solution: Page 142

22.
Not Semaphore

The ship's hairdresser had just finished setting the perms on three of her customers, when a harried man, who she recognized as the notorious gangster Ricky Roads, stumbled in from the promenade deck. He fell into a chair between two ladies under hair dryers.

"I need to lie low," he whispered hoarsely, and the hairdresser reached for the scissors.

"A little off the top?" she asked, and the don grunted in agreement.

He had not intended to have his hair trimmed while on board the luxury liner, but in his current bewildered state he would have consented to a green mullet with purple highlights.

"Have you ever considered using a moisturizer?" the shopkeeper wondered.

The crime boss said he hadn't. "Say, is there a back way out of this joint?"

"No, dear, there isn't. You know, sideburns are out of fashion this summer."

"I need to lie low," repeated the gangster. "Someone's after me."

"How interesting," replied the hairdresser, trimming. "You'll have to promise me you'll switch to a better conditioner. I'll give you a sample when you leave."

"It all started before I got on board," began Ricky. "My henchman Muggs, a man who has been on my staff for forty years, told me someone's gonna whack me during the cruise."

"What a shame!"

Ricky thought so too. "Guess they figure they can dump the body pretty easy out here."

This reminded the hairdresser of a funny story involving her cousin and an ice sculptor. Ten minutes later, the customer was able to proceed with his tale.

"Anyways, Muggs said he didn't know who the assassin was, but thought he'd probably be able to find out while on board. If he did, he wouldn't be able to come out and tell me, not without risking getting whacked himself, but he'd try and send me some kind of *signal*."

"How thoughtful!"

"He also said he had it narrowed down to three suspects. First of the lot is a passenger named Henry Marlow. A company he works for just went on the Forbes 500."

The hairdresser had seen Marlow. A distressing man with a ginger mustache. He utterly refused to listen to reason when it came to hair oil.

"Second is a chick named Judy Snodgrass. Judy won her trip by selling three dozen rain gutters last month."

"Beautiful follicles, Miss Judy has. No split ends."

"Finally, there's Jed Hamilton, on board celebrating his silver wedding anniversary."

The hairdresser was also familiar with the Hamiltons. She had not gotten a good look at Mr. Hamilton's do, but Mrs. Hamilton's bob was lovely. "So did your Mr. Muggs figure it out?"

"You betcha!" replied Ricky. "He's been sending me signals like nobody's business."

"You don't say."

"I do say! For three days the crazy ape's been sidling up to me and whapping on the deck with the heel of his shoe. He used to be in a barbershop quartet, see, and he keeps whacking out that old tune, 'Shave and a Haircut.' You know the one—tum-tum-tee-tum-tum TUM-TUM! He really lays in on the TUM-TUM."

"An oldie but goodie," said the hairdresser. "People usually knock on doors with it."

"I know. But Muggs isn't stopping with no doors. He bangs it out on my wall at night, on the breakfast table, the lunch table, the dinner table and once on the shuffleboard deck when I was trying to make an important shot—and always with that same bulbous look in his eyes. At first, I thought he might have meant *you* were the assassin."

"Now wouldn't that be a hoot!" replied the hairdresser, plying the razor.

"But I can see now you ain't. Besides, every time Muggs plays his tune he stares over at those three passengers—but they're always bunched together! I can't tell which one he's looking at."

"Now, that *is* a pain," she observed, and hit him with a gust from the blow dryer.

"I just can't figure it," lamented the don. "It's driving me to distraction, and that's why I needed to lie low. If I don't figure it out quick I'm gonna whack Muggs myself."

The hairdresser agreed that that was certainly an option. It reminded her of her sister Roxanne and the interior decorator.

"Well, you're all set, dear," she said, at the conclusion of that narrative. "Don't forget the conditioner I put out for you. And take some mousse while you're at it. Oh! And if you'd like to know who your associate is signaling about, do let me know!"

Who has the Mafioso's number?

Hint: Page 130
Solution: Page 142

23.
No Party Prank

The three sexy centerfolds—Miss October, Miss August and Miss February—gathered around the supine figure of their colleague Miss March, shot dead in the kitchen.

"It's Ida!" said Miss August, aghast. "Someone shot her!" she exclaimed. "With a gun!" she added, after a moment's hesitation.

It made for the second murder at the Centerfold Mansion in just under a month, and these things can really become a drag on a party house's reputation.

"That girl never could get on with folks," said Miss October, shaking her lovely head.

"She couldn't even get on with *me*," squeaked Miss August, blinking her pretty lashes, "and I love *ev-ery-body*."

"Who was she arguing with tonight?" asked Miss February, matter-of-factly.

"Well, I did see her yelling at poor Pamela," recalled Miss August.

"And I know she and Susan had words," remembered Miss October.

"And we all saw the set-to she had with Heather," concluded Miss February. "Well, there it is. If one of them did it, she probably waited to fire the shot when all the champagne corks were going off. Disguised the sound. Say, what's that in her hand?"

Miss October peered over the body. "Looks like a jar of honey."

"Honey is yummy," offered Miss August.

"Do you think it's a clue?" asked Miss October.

"You know what I think," said Miss August, holding up a thoughtful finger to her pouty lips.

No one answered.

"You know who I bet did the murder," said Miss August, still with pouty lips.

No one acknowledged her.

"Here's who I think did it," said Miss August, whispering her theory into Miss February's shell-like ear.

Miss February, although astonished that her friend could have a thought beyond the latest shades of lipstick, was compelled to contradict her.

She had a better thought.

Who put an end to the Ida of March?

Hint: Page 130
Solution: Page 143

24.
Further to Flick

With an audible *thud!*, Dashing Dan Paddington-Paddington-Phipps—O.B.E.—landed on the floor of the tomb of the Kweeby-Jeebie, twenty feet below the entrance to the monument.

"I'm okay!" he assured his sidekick Jensen, who had sense enough to remain back at the doorway.

"*Wh-a-a-a-t?*"

"I said I'm okay!" yelled Dan, standing and brushing himself off. He lit a torch and peered around. "I'm in the tomb of the Kweeby-Jeebie," he shouted up the wall.

"*Huh-h-h?*"

"I said—oh never mind!"

There was a thoughtful silence.

"Did you find the treasure yet?" came Jensen's friendly inquiry.

Dashing Dan was compelled to answer in the negative. "But I did find another dang clue!" he said, waggling his torch to and fro.

"You found a kangaroo? What kind of kang-a-roo-roo?"

"Another of Sir Percival's *clues!* I'll read it to you.

Half a league, half a league, half a league
onward, Paddington, and be of good cheer!
—Sir Percy, quoting fellow poet and peer.

"Is that *i-i-i-i-t?*"

"That's it," responded Dashing Dan.

"*Crap-p-p,*" said the echo.

Dan finished his survey. Besides the taunting message from Sir Percy, there were also four small mining cars on railway tracks in the room, each leading off into the murky distance. They were marked "150," "600," "750," and "825."

If Dan knew the Kweeby—and he thought he did—he presumed only one ended up at the treasure, with the other three heading off a cliff—or worse, just went round and round like those stupid amusement parks rides he knew as a child (the kind of rides he used to stand in line for all day, and were never worth the money anyway, even if he wasn't tall enough to go on the really cool rides...)

But we digress. He would have to choose wisely.

"The quote must have something to do with the numbers on the cars," he said. "I'm going to have to press my luck!"

"*What?*"

"I said I'm going to have to press my luck!"

"*Chipmunks? I hate chipmunks!*"

"Not chipmunks—luck!"

"*Oooooh,*" replied Jensen. "Hey, what happened to the kangaroo?"

Dashing Dan was no longer listening. He found Flick's clue again and studied it.

Ignoring the dead man's mockery and sticking with bare essentials, he finished his perusal and nodded.

He jumped in a cart and released the brake.

Which one did he choose?

Hint: Page 130
Solution: Page 143

25.
Getting the Goods

In a plush office overlooking the parking lot, the station manager of WXYZ-Cleveland leaned back with the tips of his fingers pressed together in thought, listening as his marketing supervisor replayed the recording of this afternoon's radio spot:

"*Heya folks! Crazy Teddy here, of Crazy Teddy's Sporting Goods Warehouse, and have I got a deal for you! It's President's Day, folks, Crazy Teddy's favorite time of the year, and everything's on sale. Bats, balls, badminton rackets—Crazy Teddy's got it all. Just get yourself down here and see why they call me Crazy Ted*—Hey, you can't come in here. I still have thirty-eight seconds left. Say, you look familiar. Oh, is that it? Well, all sales are final. What? Don't be ridiculous—Hey, where'd you get that gun? That's not one of ours, is—(BANG!) Hey! (BANG!) Ow! (BANG!) Ha, missed. (BANG!) Oo, got me that time! (BANG!) Ow, that smarts! (BANG!) Ouch, that's rough! (BANG! BANG! BANG!) Okay, okay, I'll give you store credit—(BANG!) *This is Crazy Teddy, folks, and the murderer is*—(BANG!)"

The marketing supervisor ejected the recording. "That was Crazy Teddy."

The station manager replied that he had gathered as much. "Who shot him?"

"We don't know. Apparently one of the guests for our sports show heard Teddy recording that commercial and plugged him, using the gun off the sleeping security guard in the hall. No one saw a thing, and we don't have any video in that booth. Listening to Crazy Teddy is bad enough."

"Didn't anyone hear the shots?"

"No. Apparently people have learned to tune Teddy out. The producer didn't even wake up from his nap in the booth. The police are questioning the suspects as we speak." He switched on his employer's security monitor, and pointed to the lounge. "Each had opportunity and motive. First, there's Marvin Baines, the little guy in the football jersey. Apparently ol' number four just went into the Cleveland Fantasy Football Hall of Fame. It's quite an honor. It seems he had a gripe against Crazy Teddy for once selling him a defective athletic supporter. Apparently these fantasy football sessions can get pretty intense."

"What was defective about it?"

"You don't want to know. Next is Nancy Nichols, the buff lady there in the sweat togs. Apparently Nancy's team just won first place in the Cleveland Volleyball Finals."

"People play volleyball in Cleveland?"

"Apparently. From what I gather, she's had it in for Teddy ever since he skunked her on two dozen sweatbands. From what I understand, you weren't supposed to get them moist. Finally, there's the snazzy guy in the back, all dressed in white. Lance Vasserbelt. He's the recent winner of Cleveland's International Local Polo Championship."

"Cleveland has an international polo championship?"

"A local international one, yes. Apparently the end of a polo mallet he had recently bought from Teddy came loose during a match and beaned a referee—costing Lance valuable points and greatly upsetting his horse. Lance was pretty put out."

"And one of these three gunned down Teddy in my station?"

"Apparently they did. The officer on the scene says Teddy was found grasping a map of the city of Madison's listening area. He must have tore it off the wall after the murderer fled."

"He tore a map off my station wall?"

"Apparently so, yes. At any rate, I got Crazy Teddy's partner on the line—Nutty Millard. He wants to talk to you about the commercial."

"I suppose he wants a refund?"

"Apparently not. Business has already tripled since news of the murder got out. He just wants to know if we were planning to play the commercial during drive time or not."

Who finally got their money's worth out of Teddy?

Hint: Page 130
Solution: Page 143

26.
A Lot of Trouble to Help

The upstairs maid burst into the kitchen with a chilling "Coo!"

The manor chef, scalding his hand on a pot, turned on her peevishly. "What is it this time, Judy? Can't you see I'm busy!"

She made no attempt to articulate. Instead, she took her colleague by the sleeve, and pulled him outside. Leading him across the lavish estate grounds, she stopped abruptly at the back garden.

"Coo!" she squawked again, pointing.

The chef glared at the manor butler, also present. He was standing over the body of the lady of the house, the Duchess of Wilbury—stabbed.

The chef nodded. "I see someone finally did in the old bitty. Well, if you'll excuse me, there's a poached egg in the kitchen with my name on it."

"Chef..." spoke the major-domo of the estate. As always, he exuded dignity from every pore.

"What is it, Fred?"

"I do not believe we should leave the body unattended, chef."

"Then attend it."

"We must phone the authorities."

"You can pursue no better course."

"There was also a clue found with the body. A note. I think we should give it to the police."

"Don't let me stop you," said the cook, turning to leave.

"It was found between her ladyship's fingers and reads, 'Okay, a quarter after noon, then,' as if some unnamed person was acquiescing to a prearranged appointment."

"That's how I read it," answered the chef, halfway across the patio now.

The butler and upstairs maid followed in step. "The puzzling thing is," continued the former, "her ladyship appears to have been murdered at around 10:30. A busy woman like herself would never have arrived at the rendezvous so early—and yet she clearly intended this note to be a clue."

"Have you ever tried to remove baked-on béarnaise, Fred?"

"We have made enquiries, and it appears the note was written by Miss Veronica, her ladyship's niece. It would seem the young lady had been berated by her aunt this morning for some transgression, but owing to time restraints on the Duchess's schedule, the rest of the harangue had to be put off to a later hour. This note was confirming the time."

"Well, looks like you have your woman, then..."

"If you'll excuse me for contradicting you, chef, we do not. Miss Veronica has a perfect alibi for the time of the murder."

"She was with me, chef!" squeaked the maid. "Honest, she was!"

"After her lambasting," explained the butler, "the young lady Veronica proceeded straight to our Judy."

The chef sighed. He had just remembered that he, too, had a lamb to baste. He shook his head and shed a manly tear for these unattended culinary treats.

The butler went on, "As I say, the young lady and Judy were together the whole morning. From what I understand, they spent the entire time painting each other's toenails, and swapping stories on, I believe the term is 'her nibs.' The only guests who do not have an alibi were Frederick Barbarosa, her ladyship's brother; John Lackland, her ladyship's nephew; and Mary Stuart, her ladyship's other niece. If I might make the suggestion, all three had motive, for the Duchess was a Grande Dame with many enemies in the family."

"Wretched old hag," the chef mumbled.

"Nasty one, her nibs," assented the maid.

"Indeed," conceded the butler. "You appear pensive, chef. Have you a thought?"

The culinary gumshoe peered up from his meditations. "I was just thinking. If we know who did it—and I think I do—is it really essential to tell the cops? Person did us all a favor."

The butler drew himself up. "Really, chef! Your suggestion— It is completely—" He paused. "Hmm. That is a tough one, ain't it, Ted."

For the sake of argument, who nicked her nibs?

Hint: Page 130
Solution: Page 144

27.
Good Game

"Well, there was bound to be a murder here at some point," said the housekeeper, speaking to the gamekeeper in the library of their employer, Count von Viddle. They were gazing at the Count's carcass, shot in the back by a crossbow. "It must have happened during the meeting of his wine club. Anytime you get a bunch of grown men together spitting expensive wine into little jeweled buckets, there's bound to be trouble."

"Yup," replied the gamekeeper.

"Looks like the assailant fired from the window over there. Probably pretended to leave, picked up the crossbow from your cottage and plugged the Count on the way back. That *is* a bolt from your crossbow, isn't it?"

"Yup."

"Because the police are bound to ask you about it."

"Yup."

"You might even be one of the suspects."

"Yup."

"Not that you have anything to worry about, really," said the housekeeper. "The actual suspects will all come from the Count's guest list tonight. There were three of them, you know, starting with Algernon Pundle. He brought a nice Chablis. The Count had me decant the bottles in the kitchen, and Algernon's pick was tart, but with a playful insouciance that amused me. Besides Algernon, there was also Harold Muldoon and Emile Tucker. Harold had a Petite Syrah, fruity but lacking in true body; Emile brought a bottle of Marsala, a touch cloying but not an entirely unpleasant postprandial diversion. My guess is one of them must have done it."

"Yup."

"Say, this is odd. Look here." The housekeeper drew her companion's attention to a nearby chessboard, within the outstretched reach of the murdered von Viddle. Two of the pawns had been moved: white to king four (e4); black to queen's bishop four (c5). "I wonder if the Count was trying to tell us something? It's not like he would just start playing after getting shot like that. It must be a message of some kind."

"Yup."

The housekeeper brightened. "Wouldn't it be a hoot if this identified the murderer?"

"Yup."

"It would take the heat off you, wouldn't it?"

"Yup."

"Well, you seem awfully relaxed. You figure out the murder or something?"

"Yup."

Who counted out the Count

Hint: Page 130
Solution: Page 144

28
Fashionably Dead

Backstage at the fashion show, the glamor consultant jumped from model to model, issuing her suggestions.

"Claudette, that hemline is way too long. Jacyntha, don't skip in your heels, dear. Wanda, remember, poise, darling, poise. Denise, no one is wearing scissors like that anymore."

Denise did not reply, mostly because Denise was dead.

"Well, this is no good. Girls—" The consultant clapped her hands. "Girls, there's been a murder. Denise has been stabbed with a pair of scissors."

The models, not one of whom could speak English, continued to scoot back and forth.

Wanda, originally from Guatemala, was asking the room in her native Spanish for a string of pearls to complement her silk evening gown. Jacyntha, born in the western part of Greece, was speaking Greek, specifically requesting her diamond tiara, the perfect accompaniment to her fur coat and heels. And Claudette, native of southern France, was squawking in French for the proper lipstick to offset her wool mini-dress.

The fashion consultant shook her head and glanced back at the murdered Denise, dressed in business-woman-chic with a touch of going-out-on-the-town.

A closer look revealed that she was also grasping a pair of denim blue jeans between her perfectly polished nails.

"Oh no, dear, totally the wrong look here, all wrong."

She paused. Not because the dead woman persisted in ignoring her, but because she had a thought.

"Why, I'll be. Girls, I think I can select the murderer." No one answered. "No, darling," she told another of her protégés, "not those gloves, the tan ones."

Who did in Denise?

*Hint: Page 130
Solution: Page 144*

29.
Keep on Flicking

Dashing Dan Paddington-Paddington-Phipps, O.B.E.—adventurer, Oxford professor and riddle-solver extraordinaire—stood at the entrance of a vast cavern, deep inside the tomb of the Kweeby-Jeebie. Sir Percival Flick, the original leader of this expedition, and a man Dan would forever consider his mentor and friend, had once been in these very hallowed halls himself. Dashing Dan could sense it.

"Oh crickey!" he said, still sensing it.

"Eh?" called a far-off voice, the voice of Dan's sidekick Jensen. He was still making his way through the labyrinth.

"Another blighted clue on the wall!" cried Dan, kicking at a cobweb. "You know, I believe somewhere, somehow, he is enjoying this," muttered the valiant explorer, thinking hard thoughts of his friend and mentor. "Ready, Jensen?"

"*Damn rats!*"

"Ready for another clue I said!"

"'K," answered Jensen reluctantly.

> **My dear Paddington, if you've arrived at this point without being squashed or impaled, then what can I say but carry on, old chap, you surely should have failed!**
>
> **But a pause for felicitations right now would hardly be proper. Steady thinking is still required, or you're sure to come a cropper. Look around you and consider the tiles on the floor. They'll either lead you to the moolah or through a cunning trapdoor. If you want to**

avoid a glitch in your pathway, then remember
our northern cousin and those things which
laid best "gang aft a-gley."
    —Sir Perc, from his Reflections on Mockery

Dashing Dan ground a tooth. If Sir Percy hadn't already
been murdered on his last expedition he would have killed
him himself. "Any thoughts, Jensen?"

"Damn spiders!"

"I said, any thoughts on this clue?"

"Damn lizards and things!" commented his sidekick, still
lagging behind.

It was up to Dan. He turned and allowed his torch to
play about the cavern. Other than the tunnel he had come in
through—still vibrating with the complaints of his assistant,
once again touching on the rat motif—there was only one
exit in this room. It was across a floor completely covered
in two-by-two meter tiles, some blank, others with a letter
painted on them.

Dashing Dan studied the tiles. Kicking a pebble across one of them, marked "E," he watched as a trapdoor opened and the pebble plummeted down through the lair—landing somewhere in the depths of the tomb, Dan knew not where. Cunning, very cunning.

He stepped back and pondered. From his angle at the top of the grid he could see he would not be able to traverse the expanse without knowing which letters to step on. He would have to solve Sir Percy's damn puzzle.

"Gang aft agley," he repeated. "Gang aft agley," he said again.

He looked at the tiles and back at the inscribed clue.

"Oh, you vicious bastard," he growled, and proceeded on his way.

What is the proper path?

Hint: Page 130
Solution: Page 144

30.
The Proper Key

Four representatives from Burly Movers LLC—"If You Want it Moved, You Want a Burly Man"—arrived at the recording studio fifteen minutes late. This was not a problem, however, for they had already started charging their clients half-an-hour earlier.

"Somebody need a piano moved?" asked Mr. Burly, addressing their musical counterparts: three pop musicians assembled on the other side of the stage. (He assumed they were a threesome; unless the dead guy on the floor was going to play harmony.)

"Can't you see there's been a murder!" exclaimed bass guitar, more than a little exasperated. He had a high, reedy voice, quite a contrast to his instrument.

"Moving bodies costs you overtime," replied Mr. Burly.

"We don't need it moved," explained the drummer, speaking in a loud, resonate tone. "We need to know which one of us did it."

"I suppose it has to be one of us," said lead guitar, almost at a whisper. His was a very soft-spoken manner.

"You see," continued bass guitar, "we found the body in the bathroom, drowned in the sink. He was holding this little bar of soap shaped like a piano—and, well, we think he was trying to give us a clue, maybe even tell us his killer."

"Perhaps the piano player did it," suggested Mr. Burly.

"He *was* the piano player," said drums.

"Ah."

"And a very good one too," muttered lead guitar.

"Yeah," chimed in bass guitar. "Anyway, we were wondering if he hid something in his piano, something the killer was after. I don't know. None of us knows."

"Except the killer," pointed out Mr. Burly cleverly. "Just so you know, searching the piano will cost you time-and-a-half."

During this exchange of ideas, one of the Burly associates had been trying to get his boss's attention. He motioned his employer over, and told him something that only Mr. Burly could understand. The head piano mover turned back to the musicians.

"Now, that's funny, Gino here thinks he knows who the murderer is. Of course, that'll cost you time-and-three-quarters."

Who drowned out the piano player?

Hint: Page 131
Solution: Page 145

31.
Hollywood Hit

In line at the local video store, a little old lady poked her head out from the flock of customers and tried to get a peek at the cash register. She wanted to rent her Blu-ray Discs and she wanted to rent them now.

"What's the hold up!" she snarled. "We're not moving! Why aren't we moving?" she asked the people in front of her.

There was a rumble of voices as her question traversed the length of the line. A few seconds later, a response came back. "Apparently there's been a murder," said the customer directly ahead of her.

The little old lady's face lit up. "A murder? Must mean we get a discount? Ask if we get a discount."

The question rattled along the queue again. "Apparently no discount," he answered.

The little old lady cursed. "Well, who's been murdered, then?"

Another brief wait. The customer relayed the details. "Apparently the store manager was just beaten to death with a bag of stale Co-Co-Chews."

"Never cared for Co-Co-Chews," said the little old lady disdainfully. "Hold it. The murder happened just now? Didn't anyone notice?"

The customer shook his head. "Apparently, between the sixteen movie videos, rock videos and making-of-video videos, all playing at once, no one noticed, no."

"Who are the suspects? Do we know that much?"

"Apparently not. We seem to know the motive and that's it. It appears the store manager was in possession of a rare telegram sent by Clark Gable to Betty Grable. It seems he found it in some old Hollywood memorabilia last month."

"The Grable-Gable Cable? That's worth a fortune!"

"Apparently you're right. A rival souvenir-gang killed him for it—news travels fast among Hollywood aficionados. From what I understand, the manager hid the telegram in one of the movie boxes. Unfortunately, they also believe the hitman found it and took it away with him as a rental. If it's a new release, he'll be sorry," chuckled the customer. "Those things cost you a pretty penny."

The little old lady was staring. "Are you saying the murderer has the telegram, in a movie box?"

"Apparently he does."

"And he rented the movie on his account?"

"It is apparent that he did," replied the customer.

"Then all we have to do is figure out which movie the manager stuck it in."

"An apparent solution, yes. I bet you it was a movie Clark Gable and Betty Grable starred in together. That's how I would have played it."

"Gable and Grable never appeared together on the screen," replied the old lady. She thought only real movie buffs frequented this store. "Don't you know any Hollywood history?"

The customer did not. He worked in radio.

"Doesn't matter anyway. I just heard the manager's assistant talking, and they have it narrowed down to three movies, just checked out. *Charlie Brown Thanksgiving*, *Groundhog Day* or *A Christmas Story*. It has to be one of those."

"Are there any other clues?" asked the little old lady.

For this, the customer had to return to the patrons ahead of him.

"Apparently there are," he said, having conferred with the rest of the line. "Have you noticed the song playing on the speakers overhead? It's been going for the last ten minutes."

Despite all the clamor, she had noticed this. It seemed rather long to her, now that he mentioned it.

"Well, it's the store's theme song. It's playing on that CD-changer upfront."

He pointed out the unit. The second track of the second disk in the twelve disc changer was playing over and over.

"Apparently they have it for background music in the store, something to accompany all the rock videos. Anyway, it seems after the murderer got away with the video, the manager had just enough strength to set it to repeat, and that's what's playing now. Apparently that's our clue. Of course, it's always possible the manager just really likes the song."

"You were right the first time," said the little old lady, looking for the assistant manager.

"I was?"

"Apparently," she remarked.

Inside what movie rental would the police find the valuable telegram?

Hint: Page 131
Solution: Page 145

32.
Lay Down the Law

The one honest law associate at the firm of Fibs, Windell, Hooley, Gann and Hood leaned back in his chair.

"Okay then," he told his new clients, a couple of major league umpires. "From what I gather from your statements, we have a compelling suit against the manager of the visiting ball club. Just on the surface, we have slander, character defamation, littering, creating a public disturbance and—what did you say he called you on his way back to the dugout?"

"I'd prefer not to repeat it," said the first umpire stiffly.

"Right, well, I think we should begin by..."

"I'm sorry to interrupt," said Mr. Hood. He was standing in the doorway, looking languid, yet perturbed. "I could use your assistance."

The law associate knew the partner would never have disturbed a lucrative client meeting without good reason. He followed Mr. Hood out. The umpires—basic, inquisitive souls—trailed behind.

The foursome arrived at the large conference room and discovered Mr. Fibs, another partner at the firm, slouched over a carton of sports memorabilia, a dagger in his back.

An avid collector of baseball cards—but an even greater collector of cash—he had been toying with the idea of selling a portion of his collection to the firm's new clients.

Partners Hooley and Gann had found the body. Mr. Gann had gone off to phone the police, while Mr. Hooley stood by looking thoughtful. "*Pro bono*," he muttered regretfully.

"I wonder if it was an inside job?" commented one of the umpires.

"Clearly outside," said the second one, pointing to the window.

"A bit outside," the first conceded. "Low and away if I am any judge."

"Nope. High and outside. Perp was standing on a ladder I would say. Threw the dagger just so..."

"Okay, enough of that," said Mr. Hood, looking languid and intolerant. He turned to his associate. "The reason I asked you back here is I have a meeting with Mrs. Hood at one. I need the space."

"You want us to move the body? Surely the police..."

"Never mind the police. It's not my fault Fibs got himself daggered. And besides, he only had this room till twelve. He can have it back at four."

The assembly blinked at him, shocked by the suggestion. It was a doozy—even by Mr. Hood's standards.

"It shouldn't matter anyway," said the partner. "He already had all his meetings today. Look here at the ledger. He had Mrs. Trimble first: that crazy lady who got sent up for embezzlement a few years ago."

"*Non compos*," commented Mr. Hooley.

"Then it looks like he met with Mr. Winchester, assault and battery there. Guy just got out of the pen last week. Oh, and then there was a Dr. Cobb, solicitation for prostitution. Fibs made a hash of that one too. Anyway..."

"Whoa, look at this," said one of the umpires. "Just found these in the dead guy's pocket."

He showed the group a pair of baseball cards, rookie cards for a catcher and a pitcher.

"Hey, you know what, based on this I bet I can tell you who did it. Who says we need instant replay!"

Who finished off Fibs?

Hint: Page 131
Solution: Page 145

33.
Bolted

The bookie's daunting goon trailed behind the youthful and vibrant Daisy Bolt.

The thug's air was dejected. "I'm really sorry about da trouble, Mrs. Daisy," he said, as they climbed the stairs together.

"Please don't worry yourself about it, Maurice."

"It's just, yer husband, miss, he hasn't paid up my employer, and dem bookies don't enjoy dat."

"No, I suspect they don't."

"And da last time he was over our place to talk about it, he swiped a sack of money my employer had lying out."

"I know. I gave him a good talking to about that, Maurice."

"And dat love potion he made for da boss don't work."

"I can see why you're upset."

The thug had gone over all pensive. "You a chemist too, miss? Like yer hubby?"

"I am. I write textbooks."

"Does ya really?"

"I really does."

They reached the door. Maurice hesitated. "Hey, yer husband wouldn't have skedaddled, would he? The two of ya got a place in Santa Barbara, don't ya?"

Daisy nodded. Also places in Santa Maria, Santa Cruz and Santa Fe, but she didn't mention this. "I'm sure if he skedaddled, Maurice, he would have left us some clue."

"Well, dat's nice," Maurice replied, opening the door to an empty apartment.

The only item in the entire place was a steam iron, gleaming up at them from the floor. There wasn't even a board.

"Hey, whadda ya know, he did skedaddle, and da only clue is dat iron there. Any chance you know what he means by dat, miss—Mrs. Daisy?"

Mrs. Daisy Bolt did not reply because she had already bolted to meet her husband.

Bolted where?

Hint: Page 131
Solution: Page 145

34.
Party to Murder

Miss February—dressed up as a very chic Cleopatra for the annual costume ball—took one look at the corpse crammed under the bar, and threw down her asp. Another murder! (Had the police commissioner not been a frequent guest at Centerfold Mansion, this sort of thing would have really started looking fishy.)

"What's wrong, babe?" asked Miss October, made up as a historically accurate (and sexy) Catherine the Great. "You look upset."

Miss February pointed, and Miss October frowned.

"Gee, why all the droopy faces?" asked a sexy Marie Antoinette, a.k.a. Miss August.

Miss October pointed, and Miss August moaned. "Oh drat! Who is he?"

The dead man was Barry Farnsworth, a professor of Greek and Roman history, appearing as Socrates. He had been poisoned.

"Hemlock was it?" asked Miss February ruefully.

Miss August said she had heard hemlocks were going to be shorter this year.

"Actually it looks like a poison dart got him," said Miss October. "Hey, what the—?" She reached down and retrieved a framed centerfold from the dead man's hand. "My goodness! It's me."

And *she* it was—Miss October—looking quite splendid in the pic, we might add.

Marie Antoinette gasped. "It was you!" she cried. "You killed him!"

Catherine looked at Cleopatra, and the latter took Marie in hand. "Baby doll, Miss October has been with us all night, remember?"

"Oh, right."

"And why would she want to kill a stranger dressed as Socrates? Obviously, he just grabbed her centerfold from the wall when he fell. There's a whole row of them up there."

"But why pick Miss October's?" asked the inquiring mind, still all atwitter. "Most of the others are much closer, aren't they?"

It was a good point. Too good for Miss August.

"If you want my opinion," said Miss February, "the murderer has to be one of the professors from the university. No one else knew the guy here. I don't know any of their names, but there's King Henry VIII over there eating crab puffs. He teaches Latin."

"And speaks gibberish," said Miss October, who hadn't found him a kindred spirit.

"He's talking to Anne Boleyn, who teaches Spanish."

"They make a lovely couple," said Miss August pleasantly.

"And then there's Louis XIV."

"He pinched me," whispered Miss August.

"Well, he does teach Italian and French," said Miss February. "By the way, I bet I know how it was done. The dart looks like a blow dart, probably laced here at the party. If you'll notice, the Incan warrior by the swimming pool has misplaced his blowgun."

"Maybe the Incan did it!" exclaimed Miss August.

"I doubt it," replied Miss February. "He's the police commissioner." She stood by for a moment thinking. Why a centerfold of Miss October, of all people? Why—"Oh, of course, we're looking at it all wrong!"

Who poisoned Socrates?
(And don't say the Athenians)

Hint: Page 131
Solution: Page 146

35.
In Pursuit of Flick

Dashing Dan Paddington-Paddington-Phipps, O.B.E., not feeling very dashing at the moment, stumbled to the edge of a great Kweeby-Jeebie precipice.

"Oh flapdoodle!" exclaimed the courageous explorer, peeping out over the ravine.

In front of him, leading off from his present precarious position—say that three times fast—stretched a trio of bridges, painted black, gray and white. Dan sighed and glanced around for the obligatory clue, left behind for him by that preceding explorer and irritant, Sir Percival Flick. He found it scrawled in a jaunty hand on a rock near the foot of the three bridges:

> **My dear Paddington, Paddington, Paddington, O.B.E.,**
> **Notice these three conduits, of varying degree. Two are false, one is truly paved. Such trickery, you've seen, the ancients raved. And while I cannot tell you which one you should actually brave; remember the poet, and for the nonce try and ignore that these "paths of glory lead but to the grave."**
> **—Sir Percy Flick, Explorer-Knave**

Dashing Dan moved closer to the foot of the bridges, shaking his head thoughtfully. Carefully and deliberately, he made his decision. He walked forward.

Just then, the voice of his sidekick Jensen echoed through the fog up ahead.

"Jeez, are you still fooling about with those dumb bridges. Just pick one and run across. It's fun!"

Which one should he choose?

Hint: Page 131
Solution: Page 146

36.
Law Firm Lulu

"This is beginning to become a problem," said Mr. Hood, the only remaining partner in the law firm of Fibs, Windell, Hooley, Gann and Hood, speaking to the only associate who had not resigned. They were standing in the kitchen beside the shot lawyers Hooley and Gann. "Four partners murdered in one week. Clients frown on this sort of thing."

"Uh, yes," replied the associate, tall, elegant and mentally picturing how his name would appear over the door.

Hood clicked on the speakerphone to get their ever efficient receptionist, Ms. Penelope.

"Ms. Penelope, hold all calls."

"Yes, Mr. Hood."

"And tell that slack-ass driver of mine, Dobson, to get in here."

"Yes, Mr. Hood."

"A couple more of our partners have been murdered, Ms. Penelope."

"Well, you know what Shakespeare says about that, Mr. Hood."

"That'll be all, Ms. Penelope."

"Yes, Mr. Hood." The speakerphone clicked off.

A few moments later a long, thin, supercilious man appeared, chewing a toothpick.

"Dobson, we're going to be delayed."

"Okay then."

"Someone shot Mr. Hooley and Mr. Gann."

"Okay then."

"Better find a parking space and sit tight till the police arrive."

"Okay then." The driver paused. "Does that mean I can go on break?"

"Yes, yes, go on break," said Mr. Hood impatiently. "I guess you'd better ask that new kid, Trevor, in here. The intern."

"Okay then."

The supercilious Dobson was followed by Kid Trevor, eager to please as always.

"Good afternoon, Mr. Hood!"

"Shut up, Trevor."

"Yes, Mr. Hood!"

"Trevor, there's been a couple more murders. Hooley and Gann."

"Oh no, Mr. Hood! Excellent of you to notice, Mr. Hood!"

"Dobson is going on break, so I need you to help me move the bodies. I want to make some coffee and I can't do that with a bunch of corpses lying around."

"No, indeed, Mr. Hood." The intern hesitated. "But do you think the police will like it if we move the bodies? I was reading in some excellent law books last night, and the police..."

"Oh, for goodness sakes, forget the police!" shouted Mr. Hood. "Why is everyone always blathering to me about what the police want? What about what I want? I want coffee!"

"Excellent point, Mr. Hood! Well-phrased! I'll go get a dolly, Mr. Hood."

The departure of Trevor left a mellow calm, interrupted by the associate, standing over the body of Mr. Hooley. "Take a look at this," he said.

In the dead man's grip they found the cooking instructions for a frozen shrimp crêpe. Most of the wrapper had been torn and thrown away, but the words "to heat" were still clearly visible.

"What do you think?" asked the associate.

"I've already eaten," said Mr. Hood. A couple of minutes passed, and the law partner growled. "Where is that idiot Trevor? You stay here, I'll go see what's keeping him."

The law associate continued to pore over the crêpe wrapper.

A thought had just occurred to him when gunshots rang out from the direction of Mr. Hood's office.

The law associate just nodded.

Who laid down the law partners?

Hint: Page 131
Solution: Page 146

37.
Hollywood Ending

The dull and uninvolved studio tour guide led her pack of tourists down the hall. Stifling a yawn, she pointed to a soundstage and in a voice which bespoke many long, wearying years, said—

"In here, ladies and gentlemen, you can see we have a soundstage. The makers of our films use it to stage sound. There's one of our technicians now—Mr. McDuff. Let's all wave. Yes, that'll do. Now then, if you would all gaze to your right, you will observe Ms. McGuffin's lair, the casting offices. Ms. McGuffin is obviously inside hard at work casting, so let's all look lively and move along. Up the hall, you will notice the assistant director's office, an office for the assistant director. On the right, you can see one of our editing rooms. Our film editors use this room to edit films. You won't find any piles of film today, but if you take a glance around you will notice some fine digital editing equipment on the wall, a mixer beside that, and a grisly dead guy on the floor. Now, if you will kindly step this way, ladies and gentlemen..."

A little old lady stepped forward. "That man is dead," she said.

"Yes, madam. Now, folks, if you would like to see a genuine derby hat as worn by..."

"He's been knifed repeatedly."

"Yes, and if there is time in our schedule after wardrobe," continued the tour guide, "we will stop by that comical animal wrangler, old Mr. McCormick, and I will show you all a genuine monkey."

The crowd, many of whom could do with a look at a monkey, moved along.

"Hey, here's something odd," shouted the little old lady from the editing room. "He's got two movies up on the screen, *North by Northwest* and *Rear Window.* They must be clues."

"... and here is a view of the studio cafeteria, folks. If you look hard, you might see one of your favorite bit part actors eating some soup."

"Say now," said the little old lady, rejoining the gathering. "I know who did it."

"And if you'll follow me, ladies and gentlemen, I will show you a favorite spot of mine. The bar."

Who made a mess on the cutting room floor?

Hint: Page 131
Solution: Page 146

38.
Rough Calculations

"It wasn't my coffee that killed him," said the receptionist, not on break. She was speaking into the phone, telling her friend about the murder of an accountant at her firm. "It was one of his stupid clients, you can count on it. There were three of them: Mr. Whatshisname, the blackjack dealer; Mr. Something, the BMW dealer; and Mrs. Hoitytoity, the Renoir dealer. They all stopped in today and one of them killed him. No, I didn't see who brought the poisoned coffee with them. You think I have time to sit here looking at who has poisoned coffee and who doesn't have poisoned coffee? Oh, and get this, the police found a calculator under the dead man's desk with the number 4.5825757 keyed into it. No, I have no idea what it means. They think he was trying to finger his killer, but personally I think he was working out my hourly raise—you know I deserve it. Well, I think it's about time I went on break now. Let me know if you figure it out. You already have? Well, I'm still going on break."

Who brought the tainted coffee?

Hint: Page 131
Solution: Page 146

39.
A Little Scrap

A dispute at the Watkins Association for Retired Boxers had come to blows, leaving Paul Poke out for the count. One of the club members had fatally poked Paul with the Watkins Trophy, a solid brass boxing glove awarded to the winner of the Watkins Retired Boxer Bingo Tournament. Besides doing Paul no good, it had left a large dent in the prize and knocked off the little bingo board it was holding.

The suspects were Jake (a retired middleweight), Reggie (a retired welterweight) and Frankie (a retired lightweight). Mr. Watkins, the association president, was beside himself.

"Do you think you can buff that dent out?" he asked the trophy repairman.

"It's hard to say," said the expert, smoothing his comb-over. "Could buff, could not buff. Too early in the buffing process to tell. Hey, don't you guys usually give each other belts?"

"In this instance, we give each other trophies," replied Mr. Watkins coldly.

"Belts are a lot less dangerous," said their visitor. "Now lookee hero." He pointed to an assortment of coins which had fallen out of the murdered man's hand.

Five quarters, two dimes and two pennies.

"Now, why would he be holding these? Thinking of buying something, do you think?"

"I see something with a sander," mused Mr. Watkins, still fondling the busted trophy. "Or a polisher. A sander-polisher perhaps."

The trophy man nodded absently. Mr. Watkins was free to theorize all he wanted, as long as he paid his bill. "He was probably trying to name his killer. Saw the guy coming and grabbed the only things handy. Well then, it's obvious who bashed him, ain't it?"

Who sucker-punched Paul?

Hint: Page 132
Solution: Page 147

40.
Hullabaloo for a Clue

In a lovely recreational area in Hollywood, the sun shining down on her mellowly, Deidre, that crime-loving spitfire, sat mulling things over. As usual, it fell to her to do all the thinking in the family, just as it fell to her husband Duke to wander off and make a nuisance of himself to the natives.

She actually valued the solitude. The week had been a trifle annoying. Still in search of the goods left behind by their fellow criminal Otto, they had just come from his glove factory, only to find that the counterfeiting equipment he had promised had been replaced by a sack of stolen jewels. These jewels, in turn, were to be found on condition of solving another series of infuriating puzzles.

The solutions had taken them all over the country, finally bringing them to Hollywood. Deidre was glaring at the most recent riddle now.

Looking for jewels? Ask Nathan Birnbaum.

Easy. Straightforward. And completely mystifying. She had been studying it all afternoon, and could make nothing of it.

Along with this unsolvable clue, the searchers had been given three new addresses from which to choose: an apartment in Saint Thomas, a houseboat in Saint Augustine and an office in Saint George. As if this was any help.

"Who in the world is Nathan Birnbaum?" Deidre snorted to herself. Her soliloquy was interrupted by the arrival of her husband.

Gamboling up to her side, he had a little old lady in tow. The latter was in town with her tour group, waiting for a glimpse of the new Spielberg movie which had just begun filming.

"Hey, darling," said Duke, "I found this old broad, and she says she can help."

"She knows Nathan Birnbaum, does she?"

"I thought everyone knew Nathan Birnbaum," retorted the old lady with feeling.

Where should they go?

Hint: Page 132
Solution: Page 147

41.
Flicking Along

Dangling from his fingertips, high above a canyon of jagged rocks, Dashing Dan Paddington-Paddington-Phipps, O.B.E., hailed his trusted sidekick Jensen.

"Jensen, are you up there?"

"What?"

"Can you hear me, Jensen?"

"Who's there?" wondered his assistant from above.

"It's me, you blighter! I fell down a hole. I managed to grab onto some kind of root, poking out from the side of the cavern wall, but I'm dangling over a valley of pointed rocks—stalagmites, I believe—and I'm starting to lose my grip. Jensen, are you still there?"

"Hold the line a sec."

Silence.

"Okay, I'm back," said Jensen. "Bug in hair," he explained.

Dashing Dan slid a little closer to the jagged canyon. "Jensen, I need your assistance. There are four branches opposite my present position. It appears they lead to an old rope ladder of sorts. I think I can use it to climb back up the shaft."

"Cool beans."

"But I need to know which branch to grab. Strangely enough, one is covered in frost and ice, one is dry and almost bare, another has just started budding, and the last is green and flourishing."

"Bizarre."

"I think they're painted that way, some kind of puzzle, but I don't see any key to it. I don't want to pick the wrong one, and have no way of knowing which one to choose. Do you see anything up your way?"

"Let me see. Oh yeah, right here. Ha-ha, that Sir Percy was a card."

"JENSEN!"

"Sorry, I'll slide the paper down to you."

You poor sap Paddington, if you're reading this teaser then you really are the most clumsy geezer. But to get you out of this mess, consider this riddle, I won't digress. Vivaldi is not the only patron of this tale. Now follow my reasoning and you won't fail.

Four branches near to you, we hear the poets sing. Choose only one, for three will snap, and they mean it to sting.

Choose not the branch where Keats's *joys are spoilt by use.*

Where Tennyson's thoughts turn *lightly to love,* **you must also refuse.**

For now ignore Donne, please do, and overlook the beauty which *has such grace* **more than these other two. That leaves behind an easy solution—not, not, not, now what do you got?**

—Sir Percy Flick

"He really has a way with these things, doesn't he?" said Jensen. "Dashed if I know this one, though, eh? What about you? Mr. Paddington-Paddington? Hello?"

Which one did Dashing Dan choose?
(assuming he didn't plunge into the jagged cavern first)

Hint: Page 132
Solution: Page 147

42.
Barroom Gunplay

A man riddled with gunshots staggered into a bar.

The bartender, who had seen this sort of thing before, remarked, "A quick one, mate?"

The guest, reeling a bit from his wounds, tottered over to the rail. Knocking over a box of swizzle sticks—and seriously disarranging the maraschino cherries—he managed to lay his hand on a standard pimento-stuffed olive and an almond. Sucking the pimento out of the olive, he replaced it with the almond, tossed it into a cocktail glass, and was dead.

"Everyone's a comedian," the bartender replied, and went back to his rum frappés.

An hour later, the nightly news described a shooting outside a local tavern.

The authorities were still searching for three sedans spotted near the scene of the slaying—a blue sedan with Kentucky plates; a gray sedan with California plates; and a brown sedan with Massachusetts plates. The bartender, pausing to settle a bet concerning the exact origin of the word *frappé*, went off to call in his evidence.

Who lit up the customer?

Hint: Page 132
Solution: Page 147

85

43.

Gotta Clue

A small, harried mob poured into the lobby of an office building. The gang consisted of the crooks Duke and Deidre, and a little old lady. This ever-growing group was still searching for the fortune hidden by the recently arrested fence, Otto. A previous clue had led them to this office in Saint George, actually belonging to a law firm Otto had put on retainer.

Presently, a law associate joined the rabble in the lobby. Tall and elegant, he paused in order to recite a message left for them by his incarcerated client—

"'Eureka.'"

"Pardon me," said Deidre.

"That is the extent of the message, madam. 'Eureka.' Ah yes, there was one other thing." He reached into his pocket and produced a set of three postcards. "You'll have to excuse my distraction," he explained, "three partners at my firm have just been murdered. That makes five this week."

"Only five?" asked Duke.

The law associate turned back to Deidre. "Before I forget, the money is no longer in jewels. It's a priceless art sculpture now."

Deidre shook her head and inspected the postcards.

"These supposed to connect to Otto's clue or something?" she asked.

The lawyer agreed that they were supposed to do just that.

The first card was of Boulder, CO, wishing the reader was

there. The second showed Bath, ME, and expressed greetings from Bath, ME. The third was from Intercourse, PA, and wondered if you wanted to make somethin' of it.

"Directions to your friend's various homes at these addresses are on the back of the cards. I wish I could help you further, but..."

"No, it's okay," whispered Deidre. "I got this one."

Where?

Hint: Page 132
Solution: Page 147

44.
The Long and Flicking Road

Further along his quest inside the tomb of the Kweeby-Jeebie—and getting awfully tired of it too—Dashing Dan Paddington-Paddington-Phipps, O.B.E., sighed. A fresh test of wits had presented itself.

Standing between himself and progress were five locked doors—one boarded up in planks of wood, one covered in bricks, another with iron plates, a fourth in chains, and one last one barred in steel. A plaque on the wall, written in the original Jeebie, read in translation, *"Just knock and be admitted, friend. But be sure to make your selection carefully. Disturb not the creatures four."*

The weary explorer shook his head, dislodging a portion of Kweeby-Jeebie tomb as he did so.

He pondered. The creatures four. No doubt some variety of Kweeby-Jeebie cave creature lurked behind four out of five of these doors, perhaps Jeebie-mongers or worse.

Just perfect. Kweeby roulette.

He would have to choose wisely again, and unless he was very much mistaken, some little clue, some riddle of sorts, would assist him along the way, mocking the pants off him while it did it.

He searched for this and found it pinned to the wall. A note from Flick. Clearly mocking.

> **My dear Paddington, you're on your way.
> Just solve this, hip-hip-hooray. You've seen
> the plaque and heard tell the creatures.
> Just don't fall back, or a meal of you they'll**

**feature. If you need a suggestion take this
one from me: "Others abide our question.
Thou art free."**

Dan frowned. "Well, what's *that* supposed to mean?" He
took a swig from a flask of whisky and sneered at the post
script—

**Regard the obstacles carefully, old
chum, and describe them in a single word
aloud. That will help one stand out, not to
mention make me and the poet proud.**
            —Sir Percival Flick

Still sneering, Dashing Dan described the doors aloud. He
turned and shouted these descriptions down the hall.
"You getting this, Jensen?"
"*Wha-a-a-t?*"
"I said did you get that!"
"Did I get *wha-a-a-t?*"
Dan drank from his flask. He never should have hired a
sidekick off the Internet.

Which door should they knock on?

Hint: Page 132
Solution: Page 148

45.
Elevator Courtesy

The elevator doors slid open, and a pair of television producers—a co-executive producer and an executive co-producer—stepped on.

In accordance with the universally accepted laws of elevator riding, each refrained from beginning any lengthy conversations as the car started its journey upward. They both stared forward blankly, listened politely as the tinny speaker overhead played *Light My Fire*.

Not even the corpse sprawled out between them, a dagger plunged into its back, roused any more than a grunt from the male half of the pair.

"Nice out," he said, having completed this grunt.

"Yes," said the woman.

"Lot of work to do here this week."

"Yes."

"Heaps."

"Yes."

"Dead guy there."

"Yes."

"Stan from third floor."

"Yes."

"New exec."

"Yes."

"Odd," said the man. "Suppose someone murdered him?" he asked at length. The woman shot him a glare. "Looks like rain," he quickly corrected.

"Yes."

Just then, interrupting what could well have proven excellent fodder for an exciting new reality TV show—*Elevator Banter*—the maintenance phone rang.

The woman answered it. "Yes," she said. "Yes, I see, yes." She hung up the receiver. "Maintenance," she said.

"Yes?"

"Yes. Stan called earlier. Gurgled something about murder. Man couldn't make out."

"No?"

"No."

The pair continued to stare ahead. *Light My Fire* became *Blue Suede Shoes,* or perhaps it was a little Chopin. Once again, the more gregarious male broke in with a thought.

"Lot of enemies Stan."

"Yes."

"Heaps."

"Yes."

Although neither expressed it aloud, both knew these enemies to include: Frederick, the assistant associate producer on the movie of the week *The Real Johnny Appleseed*; Alfred, the associate assistant producer on a recent Jackie Gleason marathon; and finally Crenshaw, the co-associate co-assistant co-managing supervising producer for the Saturday morning cartoon show *Henry the Eel.* They were all hard-bitten men with something to prove.

"Maintenance said one more thing," mentioned the woman.

"Oh yes?"

"Yes. He said after Stan couldn't make him understand who the murderer was, the victim selected four floors: the garage, the roof, the first and the eight."

The man nodded, keeping time to the Chopin—or possibly it was Steppenwolf. He looked over at the buttons: "G," "1," "8," and "R."

"Know who the murderer is?" he asked.

"Yes."

"Me too," said the man.

The elevator arrived, and the two alighted.

Who produced this very discourteous murder?

Hint: Page 133
Solution: Page 148

46.
Shenanigans Afoot

By the time the campus security guard arrived, the professor's office was already teeming with students hoping for a peek at some gore.

The guard muscled his way through. "Okay, what's going on here?"

The teaching assistant had matters well in hand (she was a senior, after all.)

"Someone shot the professor with an antique musket," she explained. "From the looks of it, they got it from antique musket class, but my people are still checking into that."

"The professor's been hit by a musket ball?"

"You got it. Luckily, the teach had one of those handheld computers in his shirt pocket, and that's where he took the shot."

The guard gaped. "You mean the computer deflected the bullet and saved his life!"

"No, it went right through. But get this. When the shot hit the portable, all the keys must have spronged loose—"

"Is that a word?"

"'Loose'? Sure. Anyway, the shot must have spronged all the keys because it looks like the professor scooped up three of them. And here they are: a 'u,' a 'y' and an 'r.' Funky, huh?"

The security guard rubbed his temples. He addressed the crowd gathering behind him.

"Listen, folks, not *every*-body has to do the keyboard thing, okay? You can get murdered and *not* do the keyboard thing, all right? Okay, where's the body?" he asked the TA.

The TA explained she had stuck it in the closet. Part of her job was keeping the place organized.

The guard sighed. "I see. Well, that'll probably do until the real—until the rest of the police get here. Do you have anything to add?"

"Not really. Only, it was probably one of those underclassmen who did it."

"Underclassmen?"

"Freshmen. We're on Shakespeare this week and three of them were scheduled to do recitations. One was supposed to do Prospero's exit speech from *The Tempest*—'I'll break my staff yada-yada.' Another had the 'Blow, blow, thou winter wind' from *As You Like It*. And one sap got stuck with the balcony scene from *Romeo and Juliet*—you know, 'O Romeo, Romeo, wherefore art thou Romeo, blah, blah, blah.'"

"And you think this gave one of them a motive?"

"The freshmen really hate the recitations, man. Them's your suspects, take it from me."

"Is 'them's' proper... Nevermind." The guard changed gears. "But how do the letters 'y,' 'u' and 'r' relate to any of those speeches?"

"Oo, oo, pick me!" panted the teacher's pet from the hallway.

Who took interpretive theatre too far?

Hint: Page 133
Solution: Page 148

47.
Murder, Cold and Calculated

"Oh, it's you, dear," answered the receptionist, still not on break. "Say again? Oh, you must be talking about our new murder. Seems like we have one here every week, doesn't it? Of course, you know who this hurts the most, don't you? That's right. Not that I'm complaining, mind you. I just... Oh, it was just a typical murder. It seems our new accountant, a Miss Forgethername, learned something about the last guy murdered, and was trying to blackmail the accomplice here at the firm. Whoever it was silenced her with a .38. Funny thing is, they found the same calculator lying next to her, this time with '8055' keyed in. The cops think she was trying to name the killer, like before. But if you ask me... The suspects? Well, a lowly receptionist like me is not privy to such details, but I can tell you it was either Mr. Whatsit, the sales lead on our refrigerator campaign; little Miss Whoever, who brought us the iced tea account; or Mr. Mucketymuck, our new corporate owner from Alaska. That's all I know, because as I say, I'm just a lowly... What's that? You know the murderer again? Well, do you think that makes you special or something?"

Who cleared Mrs. Forgethername off the books?

Hint: Page 133
Solution: Page 149

48.
Clue Classic

In a tiny, one-bedroom apartment above the offices of the Bath Chamber Orchestra, our fortune-hunting criminal couple Duke and Deidre, alongside a little old lady and a lawyer, stood reviewing the latest puzzle from the imprisoned Otto.

Instructed by a note to turn on the CD player—this filling the room with the pleasing sounds of Beethoven's "Moonlight" Sonata—the gang learned, also from the note, that the loot they were seeking, most recently invested in a valuable sculpture, and before that a sack of jewels, had now been used to purchase an original manuscript of the piece playing in the background.

There was a picture of the item in an old catalog of Sotheby's, valuing it at over a million dollars (an amount significantly less than Otto's original haul, but one must make allowances in the world of art).

As usual, the whereabouts of the treasure were open to debate. The manuscript, said the letter, might be found in a beach house in Palm Springs, CA; a cottage in Lake Lucerne, OH; or a bungalow in Cedar Rapids, IA.

Although the music was mellow, Deidre was not.

She sagged down in a chair, a spent force, while her husband stood admiring an oboe someone had left behind. (He wondered if it would fit in the backseat of their car.)

"Excuse me," said a newcomer—a suave little man of impeccable class and refinement. "I was looking for the offices of the Bath Chamber Orchestra. I'm arranging a function at our hotel next summer."

The little old lady pointed him to the offices downstairs. The law associate opened the door for him, and Duke picked his pocket.

The hotel manager thanked all three. "A nice performance," he added, indicating the CD.

Deidre snorted. The little old lady sneered at him, and the law associate palmed his watch.

Not shy, the manager picked up Otto's letter and read. "Ah. It's rather clear where your chum wishes you to go now, is it not?"

Where does Otto wish them?

Hint: Page 133
Solution: Page 149

49.
Flick Afoot

"Dashing" Dan Paddington-Paddington-Phipps, O.B.E., stood at the threshold of a grand hall, reeling back in giddy delight. He had nearly made it. All his struggles to wind his way through the tomb of the Kweeby-Jeebie were about to pay off. He had found the Hall of Kings, that legendary room lined in golden statues of ancient Kweeby monarchs. It was quite lovely, but beyond that, it was one of the final legs in the journey to the famed Kweeby-Jeebie treasure.

"Jensen!" he yelled to his sidekick, "we're almost there! I've found the Hall of Kings! Next stop treasure!"

"Nice," said Jensen from somewhere in the distance. "Hey, have you seen my whisky flask?"

Dashing Dan stepped forward again. He wanted to enjoy this moment. Soak up every nuance and detail. Revel in the joy of—

In a reflexive jerk, he shot backwards, just avoiding a gigantic blade which had whisked across his path. Stunned, he watched as more blades whooshed to and fro between the statues. Some darted out from walls, others through the floor or ceiling. Then, as quickly as they had appeared, they vanished.

"What ho, that was close," said Dan.

"It was sort of silver," Jensen was still shouting, "and had a lovely Islay single malt in it. Not too peaty, with just a slight hint of heather in the nose."

Dashing Dan had no time to consider misplaced whisky. (Besides, it *was* too peaty—and the nose wasn't heather at all. It was toasted marshmallows with a touch of orange rind.)

He stood and dusted himself off. According to legend, the Hall of Kings should lead almost directly to the Kweeby-Jeebie treasure. He assumed one of the three levers at the far end of the room would open some kind of door, but how to get inside. And, once there, which lever? He wondered...

As if in answer to his mental query, he noticed a note scrawled on the ancient wall. Written in the hand of that great explorer Sir Percival Flick, trailblazer and uproarious jokester, it would no doubt tell Dan all he needed to know—while playfully deriding him at the same time.

> **Enter slowly, old fruit. Life's a dignified amble, not a wild pursuit. Once you've finished your tread, observe the three knobs, but don't lose your head. Consider Pop Kipling and ponder his advice. Pull the wrong lever and those blades really do slice. After your walk one thing should remain. Remember it and *you'll be a Man, my son,* far better than any gain.**
>
> **—Percy**
>
> **P. S. Is your cousin Belinda still available? Put a good word in for me.**

Dashing Dan told himself that he could do this. Ignoring the gibbering of his associate Jensen, still regaling him from afar with his tasting notes, he crept cautiously into the great room.

Mincing ever so carefully, he passed the glimmering figures of King Weebie-Jeebie I, King Kweeby-Weebie IV, Kings Jeebie-Weebie-Kweeby I & II, and finally the statue of King Jeebie-Kweeby-Weebie-Jeebie-Weebie VII, the last of whom many experts believe was teased fairly consistently in school. Dan had reached the end of the room, and no slicing. That much was good.

The three levers, however, still presented something of a dilemma. Above the trio was the word "pro," below each a one-word label: "rege," "lege" and "grege," in that order.

Dashing Dan studied it. Latin. Dashing Dan stank at Latin. He went on studying.

Nearby, he could hear steely blades whistling along their tracks, sliding up and down inside this man-sized Kweeby-Jeebie mousetrap.

Dan studied faster. Pebbles twinkled down at his feet from above. Odd, scurrying noises made themselves heard in the offing. It was one of those great ancient tomb moments.

Dan had come to a decision. He reached out and slowly gripped—

"Hey there!" yelled the jarring voice of Jensen. "Where are ya, mate?"

Dan held off on his lever. "I'm in the room with all the statues," he replied serenely. "Just scamper right in here. The faster the better."

Which knob should Dashing Dan pull?

Hint: Page 133
Solution: Page 149

50.
Barroom Quiet

A monk walked into a bar carrying a penguin. Before the bartender could speak, the man pointed at a bottle of Green Chartreuse, left the penguin sitting at the far end of the bar, and went out the way he came. Puzzled, the bartender poured the drink.

At five o'clock, a zoologist came to collect the animal. He would have been here earlier, he explained, but the cops had held him up at the zoo. It seemed the zoo owner had been bludgeoned to death, and the police do have their little questions, don't they?

The killer was most certainly one of the zookeepers, each working a different shift. Because the body had been put on ice in the penguin cage, the authorities could not determine the exact time of the murder. Evidently there had been a witness—a monk of all things—but he had not come forward. Vows of silence and all that.

The bartender, already fifty bucks in the hole to the penguin at the pool table, clued the zoologist in on the time of the murder.

When did this cold-blooded murder take place?

Hint: Page 133
Solution: Page 150

51.
A Pawn in the Game of Murder

The gamekeeper lumbered placidly through the doorway. On the floor of the cottage he observed the carcass of one of the more peculiar and bohemian town residents, Oscar Plank. A hatchet was wedged into Oscar's midsection.

The gamekeeper knew something of the dead man. He knew Oscar spent all his time playing chess with the other artsy types who lived in the neighboring cottages. An obsessive and reclusive man, he hardly ever spoke—something the gamekeeper could respect. Day in and day out, he stayed in his cabin and beat people at chess. And now someone had murdered him.

"Yup," said the gamekeeper, assessing the situation.

"Is that all you have to say?" exclaimed the manor housekeeper. Although employed by the estate, she liked to pick up a little extra cash by tidying local cabins.

Her customers included: Roland Carson (an ice sculptor), Felipe Vazquez (a Latin dance instructor), and John Ranger (a forest ranger—John got a lot of kidding about that).

Next to the body sat a chessboard. It contained only six pieces, oddly enough all pawns.

"Think this is supposed to mean something?" asked the housekeeper.

"Yup," answered the gamekeeper.

"You think Oscar saw the killer coming and quickly arranged these pieces?"

"Yup."

"You know who axed Oscar?"

"Yup."

Who took a hatchet to the hermit?

Hint: Page 134
Solution: Page 150

52.
Snack Food Slaying

The eminent restaurant critic, J. B. Sniffwell, stepped out of his Vegas hotel room and found two room service waiters shaking their heads dolefully.

"If you are brooding over the meal you just brought me," he remarked, "then I must say I applaud your sense of personal accountability."

"Uh?" said the first waiter.

"No, it's not that," explained the second. "We just discovered our snack food manager murdered—you know, the guy who stocks the honor bars. It's a real poser."

"Surely there are others who can stick sunflower seeds in a drawer?"

"No, it's not that. We thought we knew who did it, but the clue doesn't square. From the look of it, he had been playing Texas Hold'em with some of the snack merchants. Whoever killed him must have come back after the game and let him have it with the blunt end of a vending trolley. We found him in the supply closet with the last hand still dealt out. The board shows—

"The dead guy was squeezing the Three and Six of diamonds, squeezing them real tight, like he was trying to show us something, or something. The other three hands on the table were pocket deuces, Ace-King of spades and Queen-Ten of diamonds."

Sniffwell mused on this. "Do you know the identities of the other poker players?"

"If it was his regular gang," said waiter #1, picking up where #2 had left off, "the table would have been all the regular snack food merchants—the peanut guy, the cashew fella and the chip dude. That's where we get baffled. I mean, we both play Texas Hold'em ourselves. It's pretty obvious what the dead man was trying to say with those cards, but..."

"...that's the part that doesn't make sense," continued waiter #2. "Like we said, we know what the hand means in poker, but when we apply it to the three suspects we get two culprits instead of one."

"I see your confusion," Sniffwell simpered. "Luckily I'm the perfect man to unravel it."

Who disposed of the snack food manager?

Hint: Page 134
Solution: Page 150

53.

The Game is Up

Another guest at the late Count von Viddle's country mansion lay dead, shot by a shotgun at close range. The gamekeeper found the body in the puckerbrush down by the duck pond. He called on his fellow servant, the housekeeper, for assistance.

"Yup," he said, glancing up from the body. It hadn't changed. Still dead.

The housekeeper rolled her eyes. "Not another murder! Don't these people know I have linen to fold!"

Up the long slope behind them, the shouts and laughter of various other guests could be heard. One detected the well-known chuckle of Benjamin Earl of Lupton, the guffaw of Sir Reginald Link, and the tittering of Lady Betty Leek.

The housekeeper sighed. "One of them did it, I guess?"

The gamekeeper might have replied yup, had he not paused to light his pipe instead. Shaking out the match, he noticed a book on chess on the grass near the murdered man.

Next to the body was also the dead man's own double-barreled shotgun, open or "broken" at the hinge in the middle. Laid out on the ground, it formed a perfect "L" shape.

"Another of those darn clues?" asked the housekeeper, following this train of thought.

"Yup."

"Well, I'll tell you something," she beamed. "I think I have a notion who did it this time." She whispered her guess in the gamekeeper's ear. "Well, am I right, or am I right?"

"Nope," replied the gamekeeper.

Who gunned down the guest?

Hint: Page 134
Solution: Page 150

54.
Arty Solution

The temperamental artist burst out from his studio, waving his brush.

"I cannot work with these distractions!" he declared. "This tooting, I cannot bare it!"

His agent appeared from her office across the hall. "It's the burglar alarm, Raoul! Someone's in the gallery!"

The artist went "pah," disdainfully. This was a matter for the police, not worthy of him.

"Raoul, come! You have some valuable pieces down there!"

Shaking his head, the artist followed.

A few minutes later, they arrived on the bottom floor, where they were greeted by the lifeless form of one of the gallery investors, a Mr. Barnaby. The fragments of a solid, sixteenth-century figurine lay sprinkled around him.

Stepping closer, they saw the dead man was also lying across a priceless canvas, *View of Toledo, 1597*.

"Oh my!" said Raoul's agent, gasping. "Someone has killed Mr. Barnaby! But what was he doing here, and why is he squashing that canvas?"

The artist snorted. "Another corpse! Raoul finds this tedious, very tedious."

"Raoul, a man has been murdered! And what's more, an investor! Oh my! The police must be on their way, but this is not good, not good. The other investors are going to be so upset. They were all here tonight, celebrating—Kenny from Aegean Antiquities; Roy from Rhine Relics; and Joe from Amsterdam Artifacts. Oh my, oh my! It looks like someone came at Barnaby with that figurine and he tried to fight him off with the *Toledo.*"

Raoul snorted again. "It is not that, no. The canvas tells us the murderer, does it not? How very mundane I find it. Pah," sniffed the artist again, and went back to his studio.

Who bashed Barnaby?

Hint: Page 134
Solution: Page 151

55.

Murder to Spell

The four judges in the Horace Goodletter Annual Spelling Bee gathered around the body of their host, Horace Goodletter. The murdered spelling bee magnate was lying backstage, holding a torn sheet of paper. A closer inspection revealed this to be a page from the dictionary.

"Looks like his thumb is covering one of the words," said the first judge, rolling over the body. "Hold it a sec while I scootch it down. The word under his thumb is 'preprandial.'"

"Preprandial," replied Judge #2. A meter maid by trade, she tended to wear her uniform everywhere. "Preprandial. P-r-e-p-r-a-n-d-i-a-l. Preprandial."

Judge #3 nodded. Dressed in a yellow polo shirt and impeccable white shorts, he had just been enjoying a round of golf. "Sounds like 'preprandial' to me. Nice one."

Judge #4 made it unanimous. A telephone repairman, he hadn't had a chance to change out of his jumpsuit from work yet. He could, however, endorse his associates' views. "That's how I'd spell her, yup," he agreed.

Judge #1 brought the subject back around to murder.

"I heard the whole thing. Our boss shouted, 'You've taken your last bribe, you!' And then there was a gunshot, *bang!*, and then the sound of a body hitting the stage, *kathump.*"

"Kathump," said Judge #2. "K-a-t-h-u-m-p. Kathump."

"Anyway, that's what I heard," concluded Judge #1. "One of us must have done it, huh? If only we could make sense of this clue. If only..." He paused. "Oh, hold the line, I know who did it now. I-t, it!"

Who silenced their host?

Hint: Page 135
Solution: Page 151

56.
Brain for Billiards

A pair of TV commentators stared down at the body of their neighbor, Royce Meadows.

"Guess Royce won't be attending our home billiards tourney this week, eh, Chet?"

"No, indeed, Tom, looks like the trophy will go to a new champ this time. Maybe me."

"Har-har, that's a good one. But in all seriousness, it appears someone set up a trap with this rifle here. When Royce opened the door it squeezed the trigger with this string. Clever."

"And how! Looks like the killer arranged it to ricochet off a metal beam, off the door, off that statuette and into Royce."

"Some shot, no question. Must be the work of a real lulu, this one, possibly someone from his past. Royce knew some odd and talented characters, that's for sure. According to what I've heard, he'd been a golfer, a bartender, a haberdasher, a cheese maker and a lumberjack, all before taking up nine-ball pool. That, of course, is how we knew him best. Rumor has it that he recently ran into some of his old genius gang: Theodore Firkin, Jackson Bucket and Lawrence Cord. All brilliant yet insane, a little like Royce."

"Very true. But why are you talking to me in that irritating, grandiose way, Tom, and telling me stuff I already know?"

"I don't know, Chet, why are *you* talking to *me* in that irritating, grandiose way, telling me stuff *I* already know? Hey, look at that! It looks like Royce has lined up three color swatches on the floor."

"Well, he was an interior decorator on weekends, Tom."

"Yes, but look at them. Canary, azure and raven. Look at the colors. Think nine-ball."

"Oh yes?"

"Yes. Start with that and apply the suspects. Don't you get it, Chet?"

"No, Tom, I don't."

"Well, I do. And see if I tell you!"

Who rolled over Royce?

Hint: Page 135
Solution: Page 151

57.
Barroom to Go

A bartender walked into a bar.

The hostess, who had been expecting him, put down her nail file and said, "Thank goodness you came. Follow me."

She showed him to the back office. There, jabbed in the gut with a switchblade, lay her employer, dead. He was sprawled out across his desk, gripping a bottle of gin.

"One of the Collins boys got him," she explained. "By the way, here's my résumé."

The Collins gang, notorious hooligans and very poor tippers, had apparently demanded protection money from her boss last week. He refused to kick in.

"These are my qualifications," she went on, pointing out portions of the printed page. "Education. Training. Measurements. It's all there."

"You said something about the Collins boys?"

"Oh right. Tom, Dick and Harry are their names. One of them did it, I'm sure of it. Incidentally, I can also type fourteen words a minute. Doesn't come in very handy in this job, but I thought you should know. Anyway, I've called the cops, but since you were in the same line, I thought you could help. Did I mention I can square dance? Keep it in mind."

"I will," replied the bartender, who was always looking for a hostess who could do-si-do. "But maybe first we should solve a murder."

Should he hire her—or rather, who did it?

Hint: Page 135
Solution: Page 151

58.
Spells Murder

"I knew holding a spelling bee at a biker bar was a mistake," said one of the judges, standing in the alleyway overlooking the murdered heap of one of his peers, recently thrown from a fourth story window. "I mean, you put a bunch of hoodlums in a bar, booze them up and ask them to spell good, and things are bound to go awry. Seemed like such a good idea at the time."

The suspects were all inside, back on stage and in their original positions as contestants (they were used to lineups). Hard, uncouth men, they had spelled themselves giddy for the last two hours. During the break, one of them had slipped away and gotten into an argument with the victim. Known only by their first names—their rap sheets would have more info—there was Zeke, Harry, Fred, Tom, Rufus and Bronson—in that order. So far Zeke seemed to be the standout in the competition, spelling beautifully and with the least effort.

"Hey look," said one of the other judges, pointing, "those look like the cards from the competition."

She was right. Scattered all around the body were words like "incarcerate," "larceny," "brawl," "manslaughter," and "hooligan."

The card with a recent word, "penitentiary," was still crumpled in the dead man's hand. In his other hand was a bulletin board advertisement for "*Ultimate Legal Services*, your ultimate source to get you back on the street at an ultimate discount."

"He must have torn it from the wall just before he was fatally flung from the building," said judge two.

"Curious," said judge one.

"Weird," offered a third.

"Very weird," asserted two. Her scholarly features brightened. "Oh, I see what he was driving at now. A bit unorthodox, but I'll accept it."

Who bounced the judge?

Hint: Page 135
Solution: Page 152

113

59.
The Spondulix Clue

The hard-working criminals Duke and Deidre, assisted in their efforts by an old lady, a lawyer, and a hotel manager, had traveled a long way to find their fortune. It hadn't always been easy, but it had been an education for Deidre, and Duke had picked up many nice souvenirs.

They now stood in a cottage on Lake Lucerne, Ohio. Across the room sat a small safe, just waiting to be plundered.

"This is it, honey," said Duke.

"Don't I know it," said Deidre, stepping up to the dial. She cracked her knuckles and got down to it. Several minutes later, for she was an expert cracker—of both knuckles and safes—she had the door open. "Of all the—"

Her husband looked aghast. "Watch the language, pumpkin, there's ladies present."

Deidre didn't care. She was holding another slip of paper and would have had some even choicer things to say about the owner of this slip, except there were lawyers present. "It says here that Otto, the bum, sold the manuscript and bought something even easier to fence. Says it's all explained inside."

Duke fished out a box from the safe. It consisted of a well-worn baseball cap displaying the letter "A," a jersey with the word "Athletics" stitched across it, and an envelope. He handed the envelope to his wife and put on the jersey and hat.

"Ouch!" he yelped, as the hat apparently packed quite a punch. He slid a hand up under the brim and discovered a coin. "A penny. Got me right in the coconut. That really smarts."

"Let me see that," said the lawyer. "This is not just any coin," he told them. "It's a 1955 double-stamped penny, so named because the mint accidentally stamped the date twice. Quite valuable. Just this one penny could be worth up to a thousand dollars."

"Cool," said Duke.

Deidre held up a small key and note, both from the envelope. "Says here, this key will open a vending machine Otto owns at the city commerce gazebo. Apparently it's full to the brim with valuable coins of every description. According to Otto, 'if we've come this far, we deserve every penny of it, ha-ha. But better hurry,' he says. 'The company collects the coins on Monday, the 16th.' Oh crap," said Deidre, glancing at a nice gold watch her husband had stolen her last Christmas, "that's today." She returned to Otto's note. "'You should have everything you need to find your way there. Just one other thing,' it says."

She showed them the last part of the clue.

Remember, folks, baseball's a game for the ages.
Root, root, root for the home team
—and your money, ha-ha.

"I guess we're headed for Oakland," said the lawyer.

"I hear they're filming *The Gertrude Stein Story* there," said the old lady.

"It's too easy," said Deidre.

"Easy?" asked Duke. Nothing was too easy to him. "Easy how?"

"Since when does Otto just lead us to it? Where's the ruse? The tomfoolery?"

"Maybe he didn't feel inspired," said the hotel manager.

"Even Spielberg knows when to stop making sequels," suggested the little old lady.

"No, there's something more to this," Deidre insisted. "I know it."

"Hiya, all." A large, beefy fellow, on vacation from his job as a major league umpire, loomed up in the entranceway. "Just took a summer place next door. Buddy of mine thought you were out, but I knew he had it all wrong."

Is Deidre onto something?

Hint: Page 135
Solution: Page 152

60.
Flick it Well

With a contented sigh, "Dashing" Dan Paddington-Paddington-Phipps, O.B.E., entered the treasure room of the ancient Kweeby-Jeebie.

No thanks to his sidekick Jensen—at the moment carving his initials in the wall out in the corridor—Dan had finally arrived at the Kweeby-Jeebie vault, a gigantic door made of ice. He could just make out the silhouette of that fantastic jewel-encrusted entrance on the other side.

"Just like the legend says," he whispered, placing a hand on the frozen barrier. "Oo, that's cold." He moved back and brooded over this final test of subtle intellect.

"Jensen, bring me my blowtorch."

"I thought you brought the blowtorch," replied Jensen from the corridor.

"Neither of us brought the blowtorch?"

"No blowtorch," agreed his sidekick, now chiseling the one about the farmer's daughter.

"This is not good," commented Dashing Dan, peering around the frosty tomb. "Ah. Thank goodness. Jensen, I think I've found the answer."

"Trying to concentrate," came a haughty reply.

Dan stepped to a podium in the back of the room. "The podium of keys," he observed.

The objects atop the slab were hardly your typical locksmith variety, however. They consisted of a juniper berry, a piece of licorice root and a cocoa bean. Dan, frankly nonplussed, picked up each item and studied it.

Searching, he also found a clue, written in frost on the podium.

Think fast, think Nash
—Perc

"That's it?" he exclaimed. "Four words! Four freaking words!"

The explorer took a deep breath. He pictured his happy place and was calm.

Scooping up the so-called keys, he stepped to a small slot in the wall, labeled "deposit here please" (in original Jeebie), and pondered. Any one of the "keys" could fit, but—

He thought of Nash. He thought fast—Nash, Nash, Nash. With a sigh, not at all contented now, he selected one. If he was wrong—

"Ha, finally one I know," interrupted Jensen, obscured behind the podium, reading Sir Percy's riddle.

Pick your key

Hint: Page 135
Solution: Page 152

61.
Dial M for Megabyte

Sheriff Adwick and Deputy Morrison arrived just before midnight. The housekeeper Sylvia, her lovely face pale with anguish, escorted them to her employer's study.

"Right this way," she said haltingly. "I tried not to disturb anything until you got here."

She led them down a short corridor and into a regal library steeped in dusty books and canasta trophies.

Adwick surveyed the room somberly. Unlike the rest of the house, which sparkled in its tidiness, this room had an air of disorder: papers were strewn about the floor, lamps were overturned, and the hibiscus in the corner had clearly been over-watered. Something untoward had obviously happened here.

"When did you make the discovery, ma'am?"

"Just before I called you. I came in to close the drapes and saw something sticking out. I stepped over to take a look, and, and..."

"Take your time. You said over here?"

Sylvia nodded, and the officers eased over to the spot. Deputy Morrison, catching a glimpse, quickly turned away.

Adwick eyed him coldly. "What's the matter, Deputy? Haven't you ever seen the inside of one of these things before?" Met with no response, he returned his gaze to Sylvia. "Whose computer was it, ma'am?"

"Mr. Winston's—my employer." She stepped back from the cracked pieces of plastic. "He's going to be so upset when he finds out someone smashed it like this. It's just so brutal."

"Yes, ma'am."

"His company designs them, you know. PCs, I mean. He called this one..." She fought back a tear. "The WINSTON-95000."

Adwick nodded. "Where is Mr. Winston, if you don't mind me asking?"

"He's in Madrid this week."

"Does your employer normally conduct business in the Caribbean?"

"I really don't know, Sheriff. Madrid is in Spain."

Adwick told Morrison to make a note of that. "Did the PC have any enemies you know of?"

"Enemies?"

"Anyone who might want to do the PC harm?"

"Well, I don't know. I suppose all of us got frustrated with it."

"Feelings of jealousy perhaps?"

"Jealousy, Sheriff?"

"Envy. Tending toward resentment."

"Yes, I understand. But why would we be jealous of a computer?"

"We see it all the time," Adwick replied. "Tell me more about Winston. The man."

"Oh, Mr. Winston is swell. A perfect employer."

"Looks like quite a sportsman," Adwick suggested, indicating the barrage of trophies.

"I'm not sure I'd call him a 'sportsman,' Sheriff. He's more of an intellectual really. He was something of a gambler in his youth, I've heard. Mostly cards. Canasta, crazy eights..."

"Sounds multi-faceted. Could you go over who was here tonight?"

Sylvia considered. "Well, there was Fingley. He does the gardening here."

"Kind of late in the year for gardening, isn't it?"

"Not for perennials, Sheriff. You typically plant perennials in the fall. It gives them a stronger root system."

Adwick told Morrison to take another note.

"I doubt Fingley could have done it, anyway," Sylvia continued. "I don't suppose he's ever used a PC in his life."

"I see. Anyone else here besides Fillington?"

"Fingley, Sheriff—it's Scotch. And yes, there was Roger, Mr. Winston's nephew."

"Tell me about Roger."

"He's a typical ten year old."

"Any priors?"

"No, he's a good boy. A bit high-strung, but basically well-behaved."

"Would you describe his feelings toward the PC as antagonistic?"

"Antagonistic?"

"Unfriendly. Tending toward hostile."

"Oh no. Little Roger liked the PC very much. I once caught him trying to stuff a cheese sandwich into the disk drive, but it wasn't really violent... Nothing like this."

This seemed to satisfy Adwick's curiosity for now. "Was anyone else here, ma'am?"

"Just Mr. Carter. George Carter is Mr. Winston's partner."

"I thought you said Mr. Winston was out of the country?"

"He is. George— I mean Mr. Carter was only picking up some papers. But he couldn't have done this, Sheriff. George never uses a PC. He hates them."

Adwick sniffed. He turned to his deputy. "Anything to add, Morrison? Right. That'll be all for now, ma'am. Morrison and I would like to take a look around, if that's okay?"

Once Sylvia had slipped off, Adwick puzzled over the evidence. Morrison, speaking for the first time, remarked, "What a mess," as the sheriff took out a handkerchief and picked up an object concealed in the shadows.

"A hammer?" asked Morrison.

"Probably what the perp used. Tag and bag it," he said, frowning at a fractured bit of circuit board which had once served as the machine's gizzard. "Tell me something, Morrison. Have you ever hit a PC with a hammer?" Morrison shifted his feet nervously, and Adwick patted him on the shoulder. "It's okay, Deputy, we're alone now."

"Yeah sure, lots of times."

"Right. And you know what that means. Anyone could have done this. Anyone!"

"Hey, look at this," said the deputy. He alluded to a JPEG picture displayed on the system's cracked LCD monitor. "Looks like a snapshot of some parsley, basil and thyme."

"And cilantro," added the sheriff. "Don't forget the cilantro, Morrison."

"Hey, *parsley basil, cilantro and thyme.* Ain't that a song, Sheriff?"

"I don't think so, Deputy." He studied the pic. "Herbs. But what does it all mean?"

"Maybe it was one of them cookin' computers."

"Maybe, but I don't think so. I think it's a clue, a clue to its own murder."

The deputy gasped.

"But why show a pic?" Adwick went on, pursuing this line of thinking. "Why not just tell us who did it?"

"Well, you know PCs," said Morrison. "Why do they say 'error 496' when they could just as easily tell you the mouse wire is loose?"

"Good point, Deputy. Cryptic to the last, that's PCs. At any rate, I think we should give this clue some thought. Have the boys downtown take a look at it. Oh, and on your way out, tell everyone not to leave town. I want to talk to each of them tomorrow."

The next day, the first of the suspects, Fingley the gardener, stepped into the den and found the sheriff waiting. "So, Mr. Fulham," Adwick smiled, after the man in overalls had taken a seat in the club chair beside the fireplace, "I understand you're the gardener?"

"That's right, lad. And it's Fingley, sir, Fingley the gardener."

"Whatever. People say you have never used Mr. Winston's PC?"

"You're right there, for certain. I wouldn't know the first thing about it, really."

Sheriff Adwick took another lap around the club chair, switching on the plasma TV on the wall as he did so. "Don't know the first thing, eh? Would you care to explain this video clip of you browsing the Internet, then?"

The gardener shot up. "What? I— Where'd you get that?"

"Isn't it true you're an expert with computers?"

"Well—"

"Isn't it also true that you work weekends for Winston as a high-level programmer?"

"Well—"

"Isn't it finally true that you often go berserk when you work long hours, and once, according to witnesses, were seen trying to plant this very PC in the flowerbed behind the house?"

"Yes! Yes! It's all true." The gardener was sobbing now. "I hated Winston and his blasted non-user-friendly PC! I'm glad someone hit it with a hammer!"

"Maybe you hit it with a hammer, Finch? Is that it?"

"No!"

"No?"

"No, it's Fingley. Fingley," he repeated, ginger beard bristling. "Besides, I couldn't have smashed the PC. I was upstairs in Mr. Winston's bedroom at the time. I knew Mr. Winston would be out of the country, and I was trying to get to the wee cash he has stowed in his wall safe. After that, I went to the greenhouse and checked on the tulips."

"Tulips?"

"That's right."

"I suppose you think you should plant perennials in the fall?"

"Yes, lad, I do."

"Okay, forget this line," said Adwick. "Perhaps you can help me with this." He displayed a shot of the curious JPEG on the plasma. "What do you make of that?"

"Looks like herbs to me," said Fingley.

"Is that all?"

"Very nice herbs?"

"Okay, you're free to go. Send in Mr. Winston's nephew."

A few minutes later, the child Roger came in.

"Have a seat, son. Do you know what happened here last night?"

"Yeah."

"Do you know why I asked you in here?"

"Yeah."

"Were you familiar with this PC?"

"Yeah."

"Did you smash it?"

"Nah."

"But you did play games on it?"

"Yeah."

"And it wasn't fast enough."

"Nah."

Adwick peered closer. "Maybe you did smash it. Maybe you thought with it out of the way a better PC would take its place, one that could play your games faster. Is that it?"

"Nah."

"Isn't it true you once tried to plant this PC in the flowerbed behind the house?"

"Nah."

Adwick released his grip on the chair. "Don't suppose you have anything to say about this picture of herbs?"

The child said "nah."

"Okay, fine, you can—hey, what's this?" He had caught a glimpse of a printed page sticking out from the boy's pocket, obviously a page from the laser printer in the corner.

He grabbed it and looked it over.

"'Try the last byte first' it says. But what does this mean? A 'byte' of herbs? That's not even spelled right. Did you take this from the scene of the crime?"

"Yeah."

"But you don't know what it means?"

"Nah."

"Okay, get out of here you little thug. Send in Carter."

George Carter took a seat.

"So I understand you're Winston's partner?"

"That's right."

"You don't use a computer yourself?"

"No, I've never had any use for them."

"But you do work for Harold Winston's computer company?"

"I'm Winston's business guy. I don't do the technology."

"I see. Would you say you hate computers?"

"Hate's a pretty strong word."

"Is it?" retorted Adwick. "Or is it the exact word one would use to describe a man once arrested for trying to pour maple syrup into the mainframe at the Bank of New Hampshire." With a stunning flourish, the Sheriff indicated the plasma again. A PDF newspaper article had come up on screen, and with it a photo of a younger and somewhat stickier George Carter. "Explain that!"

"It was a college prank, Sheriff. I was just trying to meet girls."

"Were you? Or were you trying to muck up any technology you came across? Morrison informs me that you smashed a bread maker in the kitchen today."

"That was an accident."

"Oh really?"

"Really. I was chasing Sylvia around the room. I was trying to get a kiss."

"The housekeeper?"

"That's right."

"She's a handsome woman."

"I've always thought so."

"So you say you didn't smash this PC?"

"Nah."

"But you are in love with Sylvia?"

"Yeah."

Adwick was beginning to weary. "Do you know anything about these herbs?"

"I prefer oregano."

"What about this message? Mean anything?"

The suspect read it over. "Hard to say. In our line a 'byte' can represent one letter."

"Can it really? Okay, Carter, I've heard all I need to hear."

Once the final suspect had left the room, Adwick went to the phone.

"Morrison, assemble everyone here tomorrow. I think I know who did it."

Whodunit?

Hint: Page 135
Solution: Page 154

Hints

1. Barroom Crawl
In barroom argot, a peel of lemon is known as a "twist."

2. Trouble with the Help
A couple of things to consider: First of all, what *do* all the names have in common? Second, a military historian would very likely think in military time. That might come in handy.

3. High Stakes Slaying
Identify the poker slang for the final card in Texas Hold'em, and you'll have your hitman.

4. Hollywood Hullabaloo
This might be a good time to look up the names of the shop owner's old acting buddies (see if they hold any other significance). Probably couldn't hurt to brush up on Mr. Wayne as well.

5. Death of Art
Just as Raoul would become famous for throwing hissy fits in local bookshops, the painter Rubens was known for one distinguishing quality in his work.

6. Classic Bravado
You wouldn't know it by looking at him, but Harry was quite the classical music buff.

7. Nod if You Know It
In baseball, every position in the field has a number (1–9), used in scoring plays. It's not as straightforward as it sounds.

8. Food for Thought

Despite what Sniffwell would have you believe, there are no easy answers here.

In order to work our way through this poser, search for an old expression for a tomato, coming from the French. Now, with that in mind, look up the ladies' first and last names.

9. Billiard Blues

In standard pool, every ball on the table, with the exception of the cue ball, has a number and one other distinguishing attribute. Pete's opponents all shared this characteristic— and one of them the character of a murderer.

10. Tundra Turnover

Look to the compass. Starting at the top and working around according to Flick's clue, what do you get?

11. A Nut at Every Party

It might be helpful to substitute variables, such as x, y, and z, for the "pecan," "macadamia" and "cashew" in the dead man's clue.

If still uncertain, drink two gin'n'tonics and call it an evening.

12. Help with the Trouble

Ponder things horticulturally. The phrase four-o'clock must mean something in the world of plants and flowers and things. Try to weed out an answer.

13. Out with the Clue

Try to figure out in what context the names Seneca and Hemlock could be used together. Once found, what variety of outerwear would likely "fit" them?

14. In Line with Flick
Start by identifying the line of poetry. Once you have the stanza from the poem in mind, look up the names of the maidens.

15. Barroom Sprawl
Ask yourself this: what's the name of the handy cocktail the murdered man was attempting to mix?

16. Hang on
Anyone who has ever called 555-Eat-Food or 555-Dog-Trim, has explored this principle, in reverse.

17. A Note of Violence
Begin with a search on Charlie Parker and his better known moniker. Next, study those suspect names again.

18. A Foodie Cooked
It's all too seldom that one gets out to enjoy period instrument concerts. Take a look at the definitions of the three instruments mentioned, just for kicks. Ah yes, and let us not forget the Boston angle. The last mystery Sniffwell solved had to do with a nickname for a tomato. If only Boston had a nickname...

19. Letter of the Law
Try covering the bottom half of the tiles with a sheet of paper, as the murdered Oz had done. It's fun. (Well, not fun exactly, but it might help solve the puzzle.)

20. Slaying in Hand
We're looking for another colorful poker nickname here, in this instance a term for an Ace-high straight.

21. Shakespeare Shenanigans
The letters, properly arranged, spell "et 2."

22. Not Semaphore
As Muggs, that lover of ancient tempos could tell you, the full line in "Shave and a Haircut" is "shave and a haircut, TWO BITS" (the last represented by the TUM-TUM).

23. No Party Prank
We don't have much to go on this time. There must be something in the names.

24. Further to Flick
Identify the poem and you'll have your answer.

25. Getting the Goods
Keep in mind that it was President's Day, and remember the map.

26. A Lot of Trouble to Help
It might be easiest to work this one backwards. Try a search on the three relatives' names and see which one relates to something in the note.

27. Good Game
The pieces are laid out to indicate a classic chess opening. Its name connects to one of the three wines. All in all, a delightful offering of murder.

28. Fashionably Dead
A search on the origin of the word denim probably wouldn't be out of place.

29. Keep on Flicking
Dialect can always be tricky, but keep in mind that this is a poem pretty much everyone has heard referenced in some manner.

30. The Proper Key

The piano player didn't just have a good ear for music, he had a good ear for the way people speak. The key to unlocking this murder can be found there. If that doesn't ring any bells, look up the clue in the dictionary. You might be surprised.

31. Hollywood Hit

A quick review of the three movie plots would be in order at this point.

32. Lay Down the Law

What's another name for the pitcher and catcher as a pair? (Not a romantic pair—a pair in the game.) (Not that they wouldn't see each other outside the game too, mind you. But just as friends.) (Maybe dinner and a movie.)

33. Bolted

Another solution found through the handy-dandy dictionary.

34. Party to Murder

What is the exact origin of the word October? Ask yourself that.

35. In Pursuit of Flick

Not as difficult as it would appear. Continue in the poetic mode. Remember the three bridges, and don't over think it.

36. Law Firm Lulu

We wrap up the law partners with a little word origin trivia. Think professions.

37. Hollywood Ending

The director of the two films would know.

38. Rough Calculations

Assume for the moment that the dead man had originally keyed in a whole number. The calculator got knocked to the floor, and his simple clue went awry. How would we arrive at 4.5825757, and what would our starting point be, the accountant's original clue? Don't be square.

39. *A Little Scrap*

A quick study of the definitions of professional lightweight, middleweight and welterweight should help you make the proper connection.

40. *Hullabaloo for a Clue*

Nathan Birnbaum was the birth name of a famous actor. Give you a hundred guesses.

41. *Flicking Along*

Involved, but not necessarily impossible. Lucky for us we have our research sources (not as good as having Jensen, but close). The poems refer to three separate themes usually found in a group of four. The one left out is the branch to take.

42. *Barroom Gunplay*

As our bartender would well know, there are all sorts of oddball labels for cocktail variations. Sometimes even the slightest alteration, like the addition of an olive stuffed with an almond instead of the standard pimento, can warrant a new name—and a vital clue in murder.

43. *Gotta Clue*

People say it all the time—or some people do anyway—but what is the actual origin of the expression "Eureka"? You'll need the whole story on this one (whether embellished or not). A dictionary should give you a start, but don't stop until you've scoured out all the details.

44. *The Long and Flicking Road*

The answer is divided into two parts. First, as always, you'll need to identify the poem. The subject is a man, a man who is sometimes referred to by a more literary nickname. Apply this to the five doors. (Don't forget the descriptions, pronounced aloud.)

45. Elevator Courtesy
Try the buttons in this order—"GR81."

46. Shenanigans Afoot
The letters this time should spell "y r u." Which of the three speechmakers, varying their lines for a modern audience, might employ this phrase (assuming they knew what all the words in their speech meant)?

47. Murder, Cold and Calculated
Still have that old calculator handy (it's better if it's an older one). Enter 8055, and give it a stare. Doesn't it rather resemble a word?

48. Clue Classic
Don't discount the background music. Its inspiration conceals an inspired treasure.

49. Flick Afoot
Nothing too out of the ordinary here. Just another poem needed to save our necks. Try looking up "rege," "lege" and "grege" first. (Suggestion: these three are typically listed together "pro rege, lege, et grege.") The actual solution will take a little consideration. Don't just match words. What lesson, according to the quoted Kipling poem, should Paddington apply to life—now that he has walked among kings? Which lever should he touch?

50. Barroom Quiet
Not surprisingly, very little is known about the secret recipe for Green Chartreuse liqueur, but a glance at a bottle— or online—should count for something.

51. A Pawn in the Game of Murder

A popular method for notating chess moves uses the letters A through H for the eight columns left to right, and numbers one through eight for the rows, counting from the bottom up.

52. Snack Food Slaying

Take the clues one by one. What is significant, from a poker point of view, about the hand the victim was trying to show? Answer: he held a six-high straight flush, an unbeatable hand in the present context. Mightn't there be a Hold'em term for that? With that in mind, why would the waiters be confused? Which two can we eliminate, from a *food* point of view? Another hard one to crack!

53. The Game is up

The clue is in the book of chess. Which piece moves in an "L" direction? Who's the only suspect who could represent that piece?

54. Arty Solution

Who painted *View of Toledo*, and what does that signify? Remember, in the world of art, a painter's name means everything—even murder.

55.   Murder to Spell
Horace clearly didn't have the murderer under his thumb.

56.   Brain for Billiards
Begin by matching the colors with something in pool. Then, as the commentator Tom suggests, match that to the suspects. A hard one to be sure! Who writes these things?

57.   Barroom to Go
Review your cocktails. And remember, this murder wasn't done by any old Tom, Dick or Harry.

58.   Spells Murder
Combine the card and the advertisement and what do you get? Well, pretty much a mangle. But work it through. And more importantly, remember the order of the contestants on stage.

59.   The Spondulix Clue
Who says treasure hidden by a riddle-spouting convict is easy to find? Not Deidre. You'll want to consult your sports almanacs for this one.

60.   Flick it Well
The poet Nash had many witty remarks, but only one that had anything to do with doing something quickly.

61.   Dial M for Megabyte
Herbs. Try the last letter first. That's all we have to say.

Solutions

1. Barroom Crawl (page 1)

The guest's clue was indicating *Olive* and a *Twist*, or, put together, *Oliver Twist*, the novel by Charles Dickens. The murderer was clearly Paul Jenkins, bookstore owner and Dickens specialist.

Apparently the two men had fallen into a bitter dispute over the terms of a lease for one of Jenkins's new outlet stores. When asked how his arrest would affect his business, Jenkins claimed it was a far, far better thing he had done; and added that he had great expectations that the industry would not have a hard time flourishing now that he had rid it of this Scrooge.

2. Trouble with the Help (page 3)

The murderer was the servant Naseby. The chef finally got the joke about the names: the colonel only hired people named for famous battles (apparently this amused him). It also provided him an amusing way to name his killer. In military time 445 reads 1645, the date of the Battle of Naseby.

As we history buffs all know—or do once we look it up in the dictionary—Naseby was the site of a decisive battle in the English Civil War, in which Oliver Cromwell's New Model Army defeated the Royalists. As far as is known, aborigines weren't involved.

3. High Stakes Slaying (page 4)

In Texas Hold'em, every player is dealt two cards face down, with five community cards eventually dealt out on the table—the board. The first three community cards are called "the flop"; then another card, "fourth street" or "the turn"; and finally the last card, "fifth street." That card's more common nickname, "the river," told the waiter all he needed to know. Teddy "Thames" was the culprit. As any experienced poker player could sympathize, Vinnie had drowned on the river.

No one seems to know the exact origin of the poker term "the river." I've asked around and the closest I can get is that it somehow relates to the original riverboat gamblers, plying their trade on those bodies of water. Strikes me as kind of thin, but that's the extent of it. For some reason, hardened gamblers just don't appear to be all that into etymology.

4. Hollywood Hullabaloo (page 5)

For one well-trained in her Hollywood history, it was immediately apparent to the little old lady that the photo of John Wayne, also known as "the Duke," referred to Arthur Wellesley, the Duke of Wellington, defeater of Napoleon at Waterloo. The gunslinger Art had slung himself into jail.

Much like Indiana Jones, the source of John Wayne's nickname was his boyhood dog, an Airedale.[1] History makes little mention of Wellington's pets.

---

[1] Munn, *John Wayne: The Man Behind the Myth.*

5. Death of Art (page 7)

The artist Rubens is synonymous with painting voluptuous nudes, giving us the term Rubenesque. The murderer was Florence, the buxom (though not necessarily nude) blonde.

6. Classic Bravado (page 9)

The note "FJH's surprise" referred to the "Surprise Symphony" by Franz Joseph Haydn, also known as plain ol' "Symphony 94." Sure enough, the guards found the baldness cure in Room 94, under the bed. They needn't have worried about anyone finding it ahead of them: if Harry's friend

Sidney had failed to discover it, it was sure to have remained there undisturbed for years, considering that none of the rooms had ever actually been cleaned.

The nickname "Surprise," originated by the English flautist Andrew Ashe, comes from a "surprisingly" loud chord at the beginning of the second movement. The composer quipped at the time that he had strategically placed it there in order to wake up the audience.[2] Quite the scamp, that Pop Haydn.

---

[2] Berger, *Anchor Guide to Orchestral Masterpieces*, p. 135.

7. Nod If You Know It (page 10)

Although it can make for some confusion, the infield positions in baseball are numbered officially as follows—(1) pitcher, (2) catcher, (3) first baseman, (4) second baseman, (5) third baseman, and (6) shortstop. The journalist's arrangement of a first baseman, shortstop and third baseman, therefore, would read "365," thus referencing the calendar printer.

This scoring system is credited to Henry Chadwick, baseball statistician and one of the first sportswriters. (It appears that Harry Wright also had something to do with its development.) For those curious why the shortstop is numbered last among the infielders, there is no definitive theory. Some say that in the early years of the sport the shortstop was actually considered an outfielder, short outfield, who moved in when needed[3]—while other students of the game just say "who cares, give me another beer."

---

[3] Dickson, *Joy of Keeping Score*, p. 22.

8. Food for Thought (page 12)

The brilliant restaurant critic—or such is how he would describe himself—recognized the culprit at once. His background in food, his brilliant background, enabled him to see that the tomato—at one time known as a "love apple" or "apple of love"—pointed to Freya Pippin. "Freya," the Norse goddess of love, and "Pippin," a type of apple.

Evidently, in the sixteenth century, the tomato was thought to be an aphrodisiac[4], hence the name *pomme d'amour* by the French, who knew a good marketing opportunity when they saw one.

---

[4] Funk, *Word Origins*, p. 179.

9. Billiard Blues (page 14)

As the commentator Chet astutely picked up, the six and fourteen were meant to signify the green-colored balls on a billiard table (the solid green six and the striped green fourteen). The murderer, therefore, must be Victor Verdi. ("Verdi," Italian for "Green" or "Greens.")

The best known Verdi, of course, is the Italian composer Giuseppe Verdi, whose name essentially translates as "Joe Green."

10. Tundra Turnover (page 15)

The seven .45 caliber bullets, taken in conjunction with the compass in Sir Percy's hand, were meant to signify seven clicks around the dial (at 45 degrees each). Using this method, one arrives at the notch for "NW," the initials of Ned Winslow, the murderer. Unfortunately for Max Cooper, this solution did not immediately suggest itself.

11. A Nut at Every Party (page 16)

A cryptogram or cipher typically uses one set of letters or symbols—in this example nuts of various types—to refer to another set, forming words. Typically there is a key, but no key is required here. Of the three potential murderers, only one name corresponds to the code "pecan, macadamia, cashew, pecan, macadamia, cashew, macadamia," or put more simply "xyzxyzy." That name is Barbara ("b" for "x/pecan," "a" for "y/macadamia" and "r" for "z/cashew"). The murderer of Reed Busby was the waitress Barbara.

12. Help with the Trouble (page 18)

As the hand behind the four-o'clock clue, it had been Sir Martin's intention to point the finger at Peruvian businessman Juan Mungo. It all came down to horticulture. "Four-o'clock" refers to the name of a specific tropical flower, so called because it typically flourishes in the late afternoon. Its more common label is "The Marvel of Peru."

13. Out with the Clue (page 20)

The reader of Otto's cryptic clue was meant to focus on the words *Seneca* and *Hemlock,* two of the famous Finger Lakes. Their cohort was pointing them to his glove factory.

Duke looked forward to picking up a few new pairs, cashmere if they had them.

14. In Line with Flick (page 22)

Drawing on that excellent Paddington-Paddington-Phipps memory, Dan did manage to recall the line from Keats's "Ode on a Grecian Urn"—"Beauty is truth, truth beauty." Such was the answer. He selected Aletheia—the Greek word for truth[5]—and the secret door slid open.

"C'mon, Jensen! The treasure is beckoning! We don't want to ignore her!"

From the depths of the jungle, his loyal sidekick uttered, *"What about my Aunt Dora?"*

---

[5] I would just like to note that I have searched extensively on the topic of Aletheia in mythology and am utterly baffled by the woman. Sometimes I see her referred to as a goddess, other times as the Greek personification of truth, and occasionally just as a sort of truth-like thing. I'm worn out. Let's just take it as given that her name meant truth to the Greeks, and leave it at that, shall we?

15. Barroom Sprawl (page 26)

The selection of vodka and orange juice refers to the cocktail known as the Screwdriver, pointing the finger at Jake Preston, the hardware store owner.

It's uncertain where this drink got its name. One popular theory, according to the International Bartender's Guide, is that its inventor originally stirred it with the only thing he had on hand, i.e. a screwdriver, and thus a new cocktail was born. As good a thought as any.

16. Hang On (page 27)

With nothing within reach but the phone, and unable to do anything into that besides gurgle, Bentley had to use the apparatus to speak for him. Substituting the numbers on the numeric keypad for the letters in the killer's name, he managed to key in his vital clue without the murderer realizing what he was doing. Of the three possible suspects, Aldrich, Beckett and Collins, only the name "Collins" corresponds to 2655467. Whether this would constitute one of the "glamorous" phone numbers the men were always fighting over, is a question for another time.

17. A Note of Violence (page 29)

The song itself had nothing to do with the murder. It was the performer. The stock boy had suddenly remembered that Charlie Parker went by the nickname "Bird." The reference was meant to finger "Bob White"—as in the common, shortened name for bobwhite quail.

18. A Foodie Cooked (page 32)

The term "flageolet," besides referring to a small, flutelike instrument (so easily confused for that woodwind by uneducated restaurant critics who wouldn't know their musical accoutrements from an egg whisk), also describes a type of French kidney bean. Set upon by frozen lamb, and with only a moment to finger the flageolet player, the restaurateur grabbed the ensemble's advertisement, together with a postcard from Boston: his notion that the common nickname "Bean Town" would stir something in one particularly brilliant customer—assuming that customer was not hampered in his efforts by some uncouth music commentator, to whom far too many undiscerning establishments are opening their doors these days.

19. Letter of the Law (page 35)

As you will recall, ladies and gentlemen of the sleuthing jury, Ozzie Windell had complained bitterly about not having enough good letters to complete viable words. This obstacle also infringed on the naming of his killer.

After he had been gunned down, the victim made do with the letters within his reach, cleverly covering the bottom half with his legal pad. When covered, the phrase he made

C	H	L	O	E		S	H	O	T		O	Z

becomes indistinguishable from another phrase, and what we may correctly interpret as

C	H	L	O	E		S	H	O	T		O	Z

20. Slaying in Hand (page 37)

In Texas Hold'em, a straight to the Ace (10 through A) is known as having "Broadway." The murderer was none other than Leadingham, the ex-Broadway performer. Like so many players, he just couldn't handle a bad beat. (Seriously, though, Queen-six!)

21. Shakespeare Shenanigans (page 39)

The student who was to play Brutus bashed the professor. The professor, it seemed, couldn't quite spell a name, but was trying to indicate with his choice of letters "et 2"—as in "Et tu Brute?"

22. Not Semaphore (page 40)

Muggs had clearly taken it for granted that his employer would remember that "two bits" used to be an expression for a quarter dollar, or 25 cents (a bit equals twelve-and-a-half cents). Although all three suspects had something to do with a significant number, only Jed Hamilton, celebrating his silver anniversary, related directly to the number 25 (silver represents the 25th wedding anniversary).

The assassin Jed was well aware what anniversary he and his wife were celebrating. (Now, if only he could remember the exact day.)

23. No Party Prank (page 43)

The name Pamela, coined by Sir Philip Sidney in *Arcadia*[6], comes from the Greek word for honey.[7] The jar of honey, therefore, told the tale. Pamela, not all that sweetly, had done in Ida. It had been Miss August's theory, in the event incorrect, that Heather must be the murderess, since honey, besides being yummy, is also made by bees from the nectar of flowers, such as heather. Not a bad slab of reasoning, and one that few of her closest friends and admirers would have thought her capable.

---

[6] *The American Heritage Dictionary.*

[7] Rifkin, *The Everything Baby Names Book.*

24. Further to Flick (page 45)

In Alfred Lord Tennyson's famous poem, "The Charge of the Light Brigade," the charge reads "Half a league, half a league, Half a league onward, All in the valley of death, Rode the *six hundred.*" Dashing Dan chose the cart marked "600" and with a resounding "Weeeeeeeeeee!", all pent-up since his early amusement park days, rattled off towards the Kweeby-Jeebie treasure.

25. Getting the Goods (page 47)

During the radio spot, Teddy mentioned that President's Day was his favorite time of the year—and, in fact, when not churning out irritating commercials, or selling the public shoddy athletic equipment, Teddy liked to brush up on his presidential history as much as the next sporting goods salesman. In that context, the map of Madison he grabbed could only really reference one thing—James Madison, the fourth president. Marvin Baines also wore the number four, and it was Marvin who took the matter of his customer dissatisfaction to a whole new level. Ire over a defective athletic supporter shouldn't really be cause for murder— but, as the station's insightful marketing guru might say— *apparently* it was.

26. *A Lot of Trouble to Help (page 50)*

Of the three names, only one had some significance pertaining to her Ladyship's note of a quarter after noon— John Lackland, the historical name of King John of England. King John was best known for introducing the Magna Carta in 1215.

27. *Good Game (page 53)*

The gamekeeper might not say much, but he knew "the Sicilian Defense" when he saw it. The murderer was Emile Tucker, bringer of the Marsala, a Sicilian wine.

28. *Fashionably Dead (page 55)*

The word denim actually comes from the city of Nîmes, in southern France—de Nîmes, hence denim. It was there that the fabric was originally developed. The murderess, therefore, was Claudette, also from southern France. Denise never should have borrowed her lipstick without asking.

29. *Keep on Flicking (page 57)*

After some consideration, Dan remembered the poet Burns, and his line "The best laid schemes o' mice an' men often go awry"—or, if Scotch, *"gang aft a-gley"* (a usage many experts believe stems from trying to write poetry after indulging in one too many single malt dinners).

Whistling a ballad from the Scottish highlands, Dan skipped lightly across the tiles marked "s-c-h-e-m-e-s," a diagonal path. He noted with some amusement those labeled "p-l-a-n-s," no doubt referencing the modern expression "best laid plans," not the poet Burns's original words. The Paddington-Paddington-Phipps are not so easily taken in.

30. The Proper Key (page 60)

In the vernacular of music, the term *piano* does not only refer to the instrument. It can also mean to play "softly," in this instance identifying the killer as the soft-spoken lead guitarist.

As Webster, not to mention Merriam, tells us, the word for the instrument piano actually comes from the Italian "pianoforte," literally meaning an instrument that can play "softly" or "loudly." It was later shorted to just "piano."

A predecessor of the modern piano is known as the "fortepiano," still used in the performance of some period music.

31. Hollywood Hit (page 62)

The little old lady recognized the Hollywood reference easily. The repeating track disc *two*, track *two*—or "2/2" out of 12—encapsulated the plot of that modern classic *Groundhog Day* a movie in which the main character relives February 2nd, over and over and over.

32. Lay Down the Law (page 65)

In baseball jargon, a pitcher and his catcher are known as "battery mates," and that was what Mr. Fibs was indicating by his card selection. Clearly another battery mate, that rascally Winchester, upgraded his assault to murder.

33. Bolted (page 67)

Although there are many fun things to know about iron, and certainly tons of things Daisy could have written about it, the only pertinent item at the moment was its symbol: Fe, taken from the original Latin name *ferrum*. The skedaddling Bolt was telling his wife to meet him in Santa Fe.

34. Party to Murder (page 69)

In ancient times, October was the eighth month, not the tenth. The centerfold plucked from the wall, therefore, was meant to incriminate the poisoned man's nemesis at the university, Henry the VIII. (Actually, his name was Melvin Dweeble.)

35. In Pursuit of Flick (page 71)

Dan quickly placed the quoted line about the paths of glory. It belonged to the poet Thomas Gray, his "Elegy in a Churchyard," and therefore pointed to the gray bridge.

36. Law Firm Lulu (page 73)

The shiftless driver Dobson was the murderer. Although Hooley tended to prefer phrases in Latin, his clue today had shifted over to the French. The word "chauffeur" comes from the French "chauffer," which means "to heat." The term was originally applied to the drivers of steam automobiles, who had to stoke the boilers as they drove.[8]

---

[8] Ciardi, *A Second Browser's Dictionary*, p. 47.

37. Hollywood Ending (page 76)

Both of the films displayed were directed by movie legend Alfred Hitchcock, and were meant to point to Ms. McGuffin, the casting director at the tour guide's studio. The word "McGuffin," coined by Hitchcock himself, refers to a plot device, specifically an item in the film all the characters are seeking.

The little old lady had sought a murderer, and she had found one.

38. Rough Calculations (page 78)

The accidental key here was the square root key, that funny little function no one ever seems to use. Working backwards,

4.5825757, multiplied by itself, equals 21, indicating Mr. Whatshisname, the dealer of blackjack, also called "twenty-one."

39. *A Little Scrap (page 79)*

Poor Paul was trying to indicate 147, the total of the coins added together—also the exact weight at which the welterweight division levels out. The killer was Reggie, the welterweight. (If only he had hit that hard during his boxing career.)

40. *Hullabaloo for a Clue (page 81)*

As any devoted film buff of the ages would know, Nathan Birnbaum was the real name of beloved actor and comedian George Burns. The clue pointed to Saint George.

41. *Flicking Along (page 83)*

Sir Percy, in his inimitable way, was describing the four seasons. Through the process of elimination, he was indicating the branch representing winter (ice-covered) as the branch to take. The other three—green for summer (Keats); bare for autumn (Donne); and budding for spring (Tennyson)—were meant to be avoided. Fortunately, Dashing Dan did make the right selection, and after kicking the frivolous Jensen in the backside, was back in the race, hot on the trail of the Kweeby-Jeebie.

42. *Barroom Gunplay (page 85)*

A green olive stuffed with an almond instead of a pimento is best known as the garnish in a drink called the Boston Bullet.[9] Based on this, the bartender suggested the police focus their search on the sedan with the Massachusetts plates.

---

[9] *The International Bartender's Guide*, p. 320.

43. *Gotta Clue (page 86)*

The expression "Eureka" comes from the ancient Greek mathematician Archimedes. Popular legend has it that he uttered this word when, stepping into his bath one evening, he discovered the theory of displacement. (Evidently he also followed up the exclamation by running around town naked,[10] which is why to this day most mathematicians prefer showers.) Familiar with the origin, and hip to the clue, Deidre could say with some authority that the next leg in their journey would be found in Bath, ME.

The girl knew her Greeks.

---

[10] Ciardi, *A Second Browser's Dictionary*, pp. 89–90.

44. The Long and Flicking Road (page 88)

The lines quoted by Sir Percy were from Matthew Arnold's poem "Shakespeare." The answer, therefore, referenced the door covered in bars. (Out loud, the word "Barred" sounds remarkably like "Bard," Shakespeare's well-known nickname.) And it was to the barred door that Dashing Dan subsequently applied the knuckle rap, Jensen having claimed a hangnail. The quest continued.

45. Elevator Courtesy (page 90)

Stan's final floor selections, "GR81," were meant to be pronounced "great one," the nickname for Jackie Gleason. Alfred, producer of the relevant TV marathon, had done the murdering, and Stan hadn't thought it too great.

46. Shenanigans Afoot (page 92)

The keys in the professor's hand—"y, r, u"—or "why are you?"—would have to identify the freshmen scheduled to do the speech from *Romeo and Juliet*. As the teacher's pet could explain in detail, the archaic word "wherefore," spoken by Juliet in that famous line from the play, does not mean "where are you?", as many have portrayed, but rather "for what reason?" or "why?" (Why is her true love a Montague?) It's soliloquy, not a request for him to show himself.

47. *Murder, Cold and Calculated (page 94)*

Miss Forgethername's message was as plain and simple as her blackmailing scheme. 8055, when presented on the LED-display of most older calculators, resembles the word "BOSS"—and therefore implicates her employer, Mr. Mucketymuck.

48. *Clue Classic (page 95)*

Beethoven's Piano Sonata 14, better known as the "Moonlight," received its nickname from H. F. L. Rellstab—a music critic who, some thirty years after the piece was composed, wrote that the sonata reminded him of moonlight on Lake Lucerne.[11] (Not technically the same one in Ohio, but close enough for our purposes here.)

The gang hurried down the back steps to the car, this race movement headed by Deidre. The hotel manager and old lady followed behind her, with the lawyer bringing up the rear. Duke, lagging behind as usual, came last with the oboe. A little music for the drive.

---

[11] Berger, Guide to Sonatas, p. 40.

49. *Flick Afoot (page 97)*

As readers of Rudyard Kipling's poem "If" will remember, the poet applauds not only the ability to keep one's head while all others are losing theirs—a good idea considering the surroundings—but also the capacity to walk among kings without losing the "common touch." That was the key to the levers. The Latin phrase represented here, "pro rege, lege et grege," often used on town seals, translates to "for the king, the law and the people." The proper lever, therefore, belonged to grege—"the people"—with whom it is so important not to lose the common touch. Dashing Dan yanked it and poured through a secret passage. Jensen followed suit (with a slight haircut.)

50. Barroom Quiet (page 100)

The bartender was able to tell the zoologist that the murder took place at or around 1:30 that afternoon, linking the murder to the zookeeper who was on shift at the time. The clue was in the Chartreuse. The secret recipe for Green Chartreuse, an ancient liqueur prepared by a sect of Carthusian monks in France, is said to contain 130 separate herbs.

51. A Pawn in the Game of Murder (page 101)

The first pawn, using the numbered files to set the order, would be on the C rank. The second file is an H, the third an A. There is a space, and then the C, H and A again. This spells "cha-cha," a type of rhythmic Spanish dance, and could only really indicate Felipe, the Latin dance instructor.

52. Snack Food Slaying (page 103)

As poker players themselves, the waiters understood what the dead man's cards were meant to signify, up to a point. In Texas Hold'em an unbeatable hand, such as the six-high straight flush held by the snack food manager, is known as "the nuts." The murderer, therefore, must either be the distributor of peanuts or cashews, and that's where the confusion came in. Sniffwell happily cleared this up. He only had to point out that a peanut is not, in fact, a nut, but rather a legume—a fact clearly known to the murdered snack expert. The cashew nut merchant—the only nut remaining—must have done the bashing, and who could blame him? The dead man probably tried to charge him three bucks for a bag of cheese doodles.

53. The Game is up (page 105)

The housekeeper's guess of Lady Betty Leek, this based on the shotgun "L" clue, was sound but incorrect. Although, on the surface, Lady Leek seemed to possess more of that letter than her two companions, she was in actuality equal in this category to the Earl of Lupton, who would have been known as "Lord Lupton." All three suspects had an L or two in their name, but only one had any relationship to the chess book clue. In chess, the knight moves in an L-shape on the board. Sir Reginald Link, the only knight among the distinguished guests, was the killer. (He hadn't appreciated the nonranked man poaching his shots earlier.)

54. Arty Solution (page 106)

View of Toledo was painted by none other than El Greco, whose name in Spanish literally means, "The Greek." The killer was Kenny, from the only company that could apply—the Greek company, Aegean Antiquities.

Evidently he and Mr. Barnaby had both come back to the gallery that night to "catalog" their investment, and Kenny had outbid his opponent with an artful skull cracking.

55. Murder to Spell (page 108)

A second look at the torn page confirmed Judge #1's theory. Rather than pointing to the word "preprandial" under his thumb, Horace was trying to indicate the word above his thumb. In any modern dictionary, the entry above (or just before) preprandial is "preppy." The murderer was Judge #3, the preppy dresser.

56. Brain for Billiards (page 109)

In nine-ball pool, one of Royce's many areas of expertise, the colors he laid out referenced the one, the two and the eight ball, respectively. Royce was trying to indicate "128." From the suspects listed, the number 128 has only one real significance—the number of cubic feet in a "cord" of wood (Royce had also been a lumberjack). Lawrence Cord was the murderer. These geniuses don't get on well with each other.

57. Barroom to Go (page 111)

As anyone in the bartending industry would know—or anyone who just likes to drink—Tom Collins is also the name of a refreshing cocktail made with gin. The murderer was Tom.

58. Spells Murder (page 112)

The murdered judge was trying to form "pen" and "ultimate" with his selections, giving us the word "penultimate." As we word scholars are well aware, penultimate has nothing to do with excellence, despite popular usage to the contrary. It means nothing more than "second from last," and therefore pointed to Rufus as the murderer, the second to last contestant lined up on stage.

59. The Spondulix Clue (page 114)

Deidre was right, the money was not in Oakland. (As Gertrude Stein herself once said, "There's no there, there"— and when she said *there*, she meant moolah.) With the help of the umpire—what a nice man—Deidre remembered that in 1955 the Athletics were in Kansas City.[12] If the gang was going to root, root, root for them properly, it was to a vending machine in KC that they would need to head.

And head they did. They arrived just before the vending company, to the delight of the criminal pair, the old lady, the lawyer, the hotel manager and a couple of nice umpires. The problem was, once the lawyer had finished counting the haul, and the umpires had reviewed his work, he estimated it to be worth no more than $9,400. A message from Otto confirmed this. It seemed it cost a lot setting up these little puzzles, not to mention selling and liquidating one's loot all the time—agent fees, etc.—and it's not like he could use the money in jail anyhow. They had a ball looking for it, though, right!

---

[12] *The Baseball Chronicle*, p. 295.

60. Flick it Well (page 117)

Acting on Jensen's instructions, and remembering Ogden Nash's "Reflections on Ice-Breaking," particularly the part about the speediness of liquor, Dan selected the juniper (actually not a berry, but a cone, used primarily in flavoring gin), and slid it into the slot.

There was a slight grinding noise, a great shudder shook through the cavern, and the ice vault slid open.

"Tally ho!" shouted the explorer. "Off to the treasure, Jensen!"

Dashing Dan could hardly contain his giddiness as he scrambled through the archway, through a series of turns, past a sign reading "This way to the goods," through a door, down a carpeted hall and finally into a tastefully furnished hotel room.

"Guk?"

A chair at the window whirled around and Dashing Dan Paddington-Paddington-Phipps found himself face to face with his old friend and nemesis, Sir Percival Flick.

"Well done, old sport! Well done!" spoke this dignified geezer.

"Guk," repeated Dan.

"Is that all you have to say, old fruit?"

"Erf?"

"Har, har. Well spoken, my lad, well spoken indeed."

"But—but aren't you dead?"

"My dear chap," replied Sir Percival Flick, springing to his feet. "Do I look dead?"

"Guk?"

"The truth is, I outsmarted my murderer in the frozen tundra. It seems both the men from the expedition were plotting my murder, so I faked my death, waited until my first would-be murderer gunned down my other would-be murderer, jumped up, performed a small judo move on the first murderer, gave both over to the authorities, and went on my merry way. Just a typical day on the expedition. Well, how are you, Paddington? Where's Jensen? Still fooling about in the hall, I guess? I've been following your progress, you know. You did very well, very well indeed. Say, how's your cousin Belinda?"

"The treasure?" Dan managed to ask.

"Ah, the treasure," said Sir Percy. "About that. The Kweeby-Jeebie are an extraordinary race, Paddington. Pranksters, every last one of them. Let's just suffice it to say, that the true treasure in life is the satisfaction of a job well done."

"No treasure?"

"Not in a monetary sense. But think of the fulfillment you've found. You went into this thing a half-wit and now look at you. Well, you made it through, at any rate. That's more than we can say for the men Sir Martin Dingle hired. They gave up on the fourth puzzle, I think. Yes, I'm quite astounded by your skill. Come, Paddington, let's bask in your accomplishments."

"No cash?" asked the gallant explorer, as the pair trailed from the room.

61. Dial M for Megabyte (page 119)

The next day, Sheriff Adwick gathered the suspects in the study once again. "You all had a motive here," he began. "Any one of you could have sneaked in here and done this. However—" He paused for significance. "None of you did. The perp, in fact, is not even present."

The audience stared blankly. Young Roger took out a yo-yo.

"You're not saying Mr. Winston did it, are you?" asked Sylvia.

The sheriff shook his head.

"No. I checked into it, and your employer was, in fact, in Madrid—which, as we all know, is nowhere near the Caribbean. No, the first clue was these herbs." He snapped the picture up on the TV again. "At first I thought of you, ma'am, because you cook—" He glanced at Carter. "You really cook. And then I thought of the gardener. But none of it fit. It was this that helped me come about the real solution. 'Try the last byte first.' As us computer experts are aware, a byte equals one letter, so what was the PC saying, then? Here's some 'herbs,' it was saying, and we should take the last byte—the 's'—and try it first. Well, what does that spell? Sherb!"

"Sherb?" said the audience.

"That is correct. Sherb—as in Sherban Young, the author."

Sylvia frowned. "But why would the author want to smash his own PC?"

"Why does anyone ever smash a PC?" offered Morrison from the background.

Adwick nodded. Sometimes even Morrison had his moments. "Don't play innocent with us, Sylvia. You all helped perpetuate this cover-up. You are all a party to this crime. You—"

The words trickled off. Across the room stood the deputy, holding a phone receiver toward the officer. "What is it, Morrison? I'm on a roll here."

Morrison looked apologetic. "I'm sorry, it's Deputy Thomas on the line. There's a problem with the station PC again. No one can get it to reboot."

Adwick turned back toward the audience. He hesitated. "As I was saying, a crime was committed here. I think we all— Well, just don't let it happen again."

On that note, Sheriff Adwick left for the precinct, reflexively sliding the hammer into his coat pocket on the way.[13]

---

[13]   No computers were harmed in the writing of this story.

Resources and Further Reading

The American Heritage Dictionary of the English Language, First Edition. Houghton Mifflin Company, 1970.

The Baseball Chronicle. Publications Intl., Ltd., Lincolnwood, IL, 2002.

Berger, Melvin. *Anchor Guide to Orchestral Masterpieces.* Anchor Books, New York, 1995.

Berger, Melvin. *Guide to Sonatas.* Anchor Books, New York, 1991.

Ciardi, John. *A Browser's Dictionary.* Akadine Press, New York, 1997.

Ciardi, John. *A Second Browser's Dictionary.* Akadine Press, New York, 1997.

Dickson, Paul. *Joy of Keeping Score.* Walker, New York, 1996.

Funk, Wilfred. *Word Origins and their Romantic Stories.* Grosset & Dunlap, New York, 1950.

International Bartender's Guide. Random House, New York, 1997.

Internet Movie Database (www.imdb.com)

Janson, H. W. *History of Art.* Harry N. Abrams, New York, 1970.

Merriam-Webster Collegiate Dictionary (Online edition). Merriam-Webster, 2006.

Merriam-Webster Unabridged Dictionary (Online edition). Merriam-Webster, 2006.

Munn, Michael. *John Wayne: The Man Behind the Myth* (Kindle edition). Penguin, 2008.

New Oxford American Dictionary (Electronic edition, Kindle/Apple). Oxford University Press, Inc., 2005.

Random House Webster's Unabridged Dictionary, Second Edition. Random House, New York, 1997.

Rifkin, June. *The Everything Baby Names Book.* Adams Media, Avon, Massachusetts, 2006.

Wikipedia, The Free Encyclopedia (www.wikipedia.org)

About the Author

Sherban Young splits his time between Maryland and Maine, and as a writer of humorous mystery novels, has been called the next P. G. Wodehouse, or at the very least, the current Sherban Young. He has an encyclopedic knowledge of literature, classical music, baseball, and film (although it should be noted that this encyclopedia is a single volume, pop-up book edition). When he isn't working on a new novel, or an incredibly clever puzzle book, he enjoys single malt, poker, billiards, his MINI Cooper, and listing things he enjoys.

A CATALOG OF SELECTED
DOVER BOOKS
IN ALL FIELDS OF INTEREST

A CATALOG OF SELECTED DOVER
BOOKS IN ALL FIELDS OF INTEREST

100 BEST-LOVED POEMS, Edited by Philip Smith. "The Passionate Shepherd to His Love," "Shall I compare thee to a summer's day?" "Death, be not proud," "The Raven," "The Road Not Taken," plus works by Blake, Wordsworth, Byron, Shelley, Keats, many others. 96pp. 5 3/16 x 8 1/4.   0-486-28553-7

100 SMALL HOUSES OF THE THIRTIES, Brown-Blodgett Company. Exterior photographs and floor plans for 100 charming structures. Illustrations of models accompanied by descriptions of interiors, color schemes, closet space, and other amenities. 200 illustrations. 112pp. 8 3/8 x 11.   0-486-44131-8

1000 TURN-OF-THE-CENTURY HOUSES: With Illustrations and Floor Plans, Herbert C. Chivers. Reproduced from a rare edition, this showcase of homes ranges from cottages and bungalows to sprawling mansions. Each house is meticulously illustrated and accompanied by complete floor plans. 256pp. 9 3/8 x 12 1/4.

     0-486-45596-3

101 GREAT AMERICAN POEMS, Edited by The American Poetry & Literacy Project. Rich treasury of verse from the 19th and 20th centuries includes works by Edgar Allan Poe, Robert Frost, Walt Whitman, Langston Hughes, Emily Dickinson, T. S. Eliot, other notables. 96pp. 5 3/16 x 8 1/4.   0-486-40158-8

101 GREAT SAMURAI PRINTS, Utagawa Kuniyoshi. Kuniyoshi was a master of the warrior woodblock print — and these 18th-century illustrations represent the pinnacle of his craft. Full-color portraits of renowned Japanese samurais pulse with movement, passion, and remarkably fine detail. 112pp. 8 3/8 x 11.   0-486-46523-3

ABC OF BALLET, Janet Grosser. Clearly worded, abundantly illustrated little guide defines basic ballet-related terms: arabesque, battement, pas de chat, relevé, sissonne, many others. Pronunciation guide included. Excellent primer. 48pp. 4 3/16 x 5 3/4.

     0-486-40871-X

ACCESSORIES OF DRESS: An Illustrated Encyclopedia, Katherine Lester and Bess Viola Oerke. Illustrations of hats, veils, wigs, cravats, shawls, shoes, gloves, and other accessories enhance an engaging commentary that reveals the humor and charm of the many-sided story of accessorized apparel. 644 figures and 59 plates. 608pp. 6 1/8 x 9 1/4.

     0-486-43378-1

ADVENTURES OF HUCKLEBERRY FINN, Mark Twain. Join Huck and Jim as their boyhood adventures along the Mississippi River lead them into a world of excitement, danger, and self-discovery. Humorous narrative, lyrical descriptions of the Mississippi valley, and memorable characters. 224pp. 5 3/16 x 8 1/4.   0-486-28061-6

ALICE STARMORE'S BOOK OF FAIR ISLE KNITTING, Alice Starmore. A noted designer from the region of Scotland's Fair Isle explores the history and techniques of this distinctive, stranded-color knitting style and provides copious illustrated instructions for 14 original knitwear designs. 208pp. 8 3/8 x 10 7/8.   0-486-47218-3

Browse over 9,000 books at www.doverpublications.com

CATALOG OF DOVER BOOKS

ALICE'S ADVENTURES IN WONDERLAND, Lewis Carroll. Beloved classic about a little girl lost in a topsy-turvy land and her encounters with the White Rabbit, March Hare, Mad Hatter, Cheshire Cat, and other delightfully improbable characters. 42 illustrations by Sir John Tenniel. 96pp. 5³⁄₁₆ x 8¼.   0-486-27543-4

AMERICA'S LIGHTHOUSES: An Illustrated History, Francis Ross Holland. Profusely illustrated fact-filled survey of American lighthouses since 1716. Over 200 stations — East, Gulf, and West coasts, Great Lakes, Hawaii, Alaska, Puerto Rico, the Virgin Islands, and the Mississippi and St. Lawrence Rivers. 240pp. 8 x 10¾.
        0-486-25576-X

AN ENCYCLOPEDIA OF THE VIOLIN, Alberto Bachmann. Translated by Frederick H. Martens. Introduction by Eugene Ysaye. First published in 1925, this renowned reference remains unsurpassed as a source of essential information, from construction and evolution to repertoire and technique. Includes a glossary and 73 illustrations. 496pp. 6⅛ x 9¼.   0-486-46618-3

ANIMALS: 1,419 Copyright-Free Illustrations of Mammals, Birds, Fish, Insects, etc., Selected by Jim Harter. Selected for its visual impact and ease of use, this outstanding collection of wood engravings presents over 1,000 species of animals in extremely lifelike poses. Includes mammals, birds, reptiles, amphibians, fish, insects, and other invertebrates. 284pp. 9 x 12.   0-486-23766-4

THE ANNALS, Tacitus. Translated by Alfred John Church and William Jackson Brodribb. This vital chronicle of Imperial Rome, written by the era's great historian, spans A.D. 14-68 and paints incisive psychological portraits of major figures, from Tiberius to Nero. 416pp. 5³⁄₁₆ x 8¼.   0-486-45236-0

ANTIGONE, Sophocles. Filled with passionate speeches and sensitive probing of moral and philosophical issues, this powerful and often-performed Greek drama reveals the grim fate that befalls the children of Oedipus. Footnotes. 64pp. 5³⁄₁₆ x 8 ¼.   0-486-27804-2

ART DECO DECORATIVE PATTERNS IN FULL COLOR, Christian Stoll. Reprinted from a rare 1910 portfolio, 160 sensuous and exotic images depict a breathtaking array of florals, geometrics, and abstracts — all elegant in their stark simplicity. 64pp. 8⅜ x 11.   0-486-44862-2

THE ARTHUR RACKHAM TREASURY: 86 Full-Color Illustrations, Arthur Rackham. Selected and Edited by Jeff A. Menges. A stunning treasury of 86 full-page plates span the famed English artist's career, from *Rip Van Winkle* (1905) to masterworks such as *Undine, A Midsummer Night's Dream,* and *Wind in the Willows* (1939). 96pp. 8⅜ x 11.
        0-486-44685-9

THE AUTHENTIC GILBERT & SULLIVAN SONGBOOK, W. S. Gilbert and A. S. Sullivan. The most comprehensive collection available, this songbook includes selections from every one of Gilbert and Sullivan's light operas. Ninety-two numbers are presented uncut and unedited, and in their original keys. 410pp. 9 x 12.
        0-486-23482-7

THE AWAKENING, Kate Chopin. First published in 1899, this controversial novel of a New Orleans wife's search for love outside a stifling marriage shocked readers. Today, it remains a first-rate narrative with superb characterization. New introductory Note. 128pp. 5³⁄₁₆ x 8¼.   0-486-27786-0

BASIC DRAWING, Louis Priscilla. Beginning with perspective, this commonsense manual progresses to the figure in movement, light and shade, anatomy, drapery, composition, trees and landscape, and outdoor sketching. Black-and-white illustrations throughout. 128pp. 8⅜ x 11.   0-486-45815-0

THE BATTLES THAT CHANGED HISTORY, Fletcher Pratt. Historian profiles 16 crucial conflicts, ancient to modern, that changed the course of Western civilization. Gripping accounts of battles led by Alexander the Great, Joan of Arc, Ulysses S. Grant, other commanders. 27 maps. 352pp. 5⅜ x 8½.   0-486-41129-X

BEETHOVEN'S LETTERS, Ludwig van Beethoven. Edited by Dr. A. C. Kalischer. Features 457 letters to fellow musicians, friends, greats, patrons, and literary men. Reveals musical thoughts, quirks of personality, insights, and daily events. Includes 15 plates. 410pp. 5⅜ x 8½.   0-486-22769-3

BERNICE BOBS HER HAIR AND OTHER STORIES, F. Scott Fitzgerald. This brilliant anthology includes 6 of Fitzgerald's most popular stories: "The Diamond as Big as the Ritz," the title tale, "The Offshore Pirate," "The Ice Palace," "The Jelly Bean," and "May Day." 176pp. 5⅜ x 8½.   0-486-47049-0

BESLER'S BOOK OF FLOWERS AND PLANTS: 73 Full-Color Plates from Hortus Eystettensis, 1613, Basilius Besler. Here is a selection of magnificent plates from the *Hortus Eystettensis,* which vividly illustrated and identified the plants, flowers, and trees that thrived in the legendary German garden at Eichstätt. 80pp. 8⅜ x 11.
0-486-46005-3

THE BOOK OF KELLS, Edited by Blanche Cirker. Painstakingly reproduced from a rare facsimile edition, this volume contains full-page decorations, portraits, illustrations, plus a sampling of textual leaves with exquisite calligraphy and ornamentation. 32 full-color illustrations. 32pp. 9⅜ x 12¼.   0-486-24345-1

THE BOOK OF THE CROSSBOW: With an Additional Section on Catapults and Other Siege Engines, Ralph Payne-Gallwey. Fascinating study traces history and use of crossbow as military and sporting weapon, from Middle Ages to modern times. Also covers related weapons: balistas, catapults, Turkish bows, more. Over 240 illustrations. 400pp. 7¼ x 10⅛.   0-486-28720-3

THE BUNGALOW BOOK: Floor Plans and Photos of 112 Houses, 1910, Henry L. Wilson. Here are 112 of the most popular and economic blueprints of the early 20th century — plus an illustration or photograph of each completed house. A wonderful time capsule that still offers a wealth of valuable insights. 160pp. 8⅜ x 11.
0-486-45104-6

THE CALL OF THE WILD, Jack London. A classic novel of adventure, drawn from London's own experiences as a Klondike adventurer, relating the story of a heroic dog caught in the brutal life of the Alaska Gold Rush. Note. 64pp. 5³⁄₁₆ x 8¼.
0-486-26472-6

CANDIDE, Voltaire. Edited by Francois-Marie Arouet. One of the world's great satires since its first publication in 1759. Witty, caustic skewering of romance, science, philosophy, religion, government — nearly all human ideals and institutions. 112pp. 5³⁄₁₆ x 8¼.   0-486-26689-3

CELEBRATED IN THEIR TIME: Photographic Portraits from the George Grantham Bain Collection, Edited by Amy Pastan. With an Introduction by Michael Carlebach. Remarkable portrait gallery features 112 rare images of Albert Einstein, Charlie Chaplin, the Wright Brothers, Henry Ford, and other luminaries from the worlds of politics, art, entertainment, and industry. 128pp. 8⅜ x 11.   0-486-46754-6

CHARIOTS FOR APOLLO: The NASA History of Manned Lunar Spacecraft to 1969, Courtney G. Brooks, James M. Grimwood, and Loyd S. Swenson, Jr. This illustrated history by a trio of experts is the definitive reference on the Apollo spacecraft and lunar modules. It traces the vehicles' design, development, and operation in space. More than 100 photographs and illustrations. 576pp. 6¾ x 9¼. 0-486-46756-2

A CHRISTMAS CAROL, Charles Dickens. This engrossing tale relates Ebenezer Scrooge's ghostly journeys through Christmases past, present, and future and his ultimate transformation from a harsh and grasping old miser to a charitable and compassionate human being. 80pp. 5³⁄₁₆ x 8¼. 0-486-26865-9

COMMON SENSE, Thomas Paine. First published in January of 1776, this highly influential landmark document clearly and persuasively argued for American separation from Great Britain and paved the way for the Declaration of Independence. 64pp. 5³⁄₁₆ x 8¼. 0-486-29602-4

THE COMPLETE SHORT STORIES OF OSCAR WILDE, Oscar Wilde. Complete texts of "The Happy Prince and Other Tales," "A House of Pomegranates," "Lord Arthur Savile's Crime and Other Stories," "Poems in Prose," and "The Portrait of Mr. W. H." 208pp. 5³⁄₁₆ x 8¼. 0-486-45216-6

COMPLETE SONNETS, William Shakespeare. Over 150 exquisite poems deal with love, friendship, the tyranny of time, beauty's evanescence, death, and other themes in language of remarkable power, precision, and beauty. Glossary of archaic terms. 80pp. 5³⁄₁₆ x 8¼. 0-486-26686-9

THE COUNT OF MONTE CRISTO: Abridged Edition, Alexandre Dumas. Falsely accused of treason, Edmond Dantès is imprisoned in the bleak Chateau d'If. After a hair-raising escape, he launches an elaborate plot to extract a bitter revenge against those who betrayed him. 448pp. 5³⁄₁₆ x 8¼. 0-486-45643-9

CRAFTSMAN BUNGALOWS: Designs from the Pacific Northwest, Yoho & Merritt. This reprint of a rare catalog, showcasing the charming simplicity and cozy style of Craftsman bungalows, is filled with photos of completed homes, plus floor plans and estimated costs. An indispensable resource for architects, historians, and illustrators. 112pp. 10 x 7. 0-486-46875-5

CRAFTSMAN BUNGALOWS: 59 Homes from "The Craftsman," Edited by Gustav Stickley. Best and most attractive designs from Arts and Crafts Movement publication — 1903–1916 — includes sketches, photographs of homes, floor plans, descriptive text. 128pp. 8¼ x 11. 0-486-25829-7

CRIME AND PUNISHMENT, Fyodor Dostoyevsky. Translated by Constance Garnett. Supreme masterpiece tells the story of Raskolnikov, a student tormented by his own thoughts after he murders an old woman. Overwhelmed by guilt and terror, he confesses and goes to prison. 480pp. 5³⁄₁₆ x 8¼. 0-486-41587-2

THE DECLARATION OF INDEPENDENCE AND OTHER GREAT DOCUMENTS OF AMERICAN HISTORY: 1775-1865, Edited by John Grafton. Thirteen compelling and influential documents: Henry's "Give Me Liberty or Give Me Death," Declaration of Independence, The Constitution, Washington's First Inaugural Address, The Monroe Doctrine, The Emancipation Proclamation, Gettysburg Address, more. 64pp. 5³⁄₁₆ x 8¼. 0-486-41124-9

THE DESERT AND THE SOWN: Travels in Palestine and Syria, Gertrude Bell. "The female Lawrence of Arabia," Gertrude Bell wrote captivating, perceptive accounts of her travels in the Middle East. This intriguing narrative, accompanied by 160 photos, traces her 1905 sojourn in Lebanon, Syria, and Palestine. 368pp. 5⅜ x 8½. 0-486-46876-3

A DOLL'S HOUSE, Henrik Ibsen. Ibsen's best-known play displays his genius for realistic prose drama. An expression of women's rights, the play climaxes when the central character, Nora, rejects a smothering marriage and life in "a doll's house." 80pp. 5³⁄₁₆ x 8¼. 0-486-27062-9

DOOMED SHIPS: Great Ocean Liner Disasters, William H. Miller, Jr. Nearly 200 photographs, many from private collections, highlight tales of some of the vessels whose pleasure cruises ended in catastrophe: the *Morro Castle, Normandie, Andrea Doria, Europa,* and many others. 128pp. 8⅜ x 11¾. 0-486-45366-9

THE DORÉ BIBLE ILLUSTRATIONS, Gustave Doré. Detailed plates from the Bible: the Creation scenes, Adam and Eve, horrifying visions of the Flood, the battle sequences with their monumental crowds, depictions of the life of Jesus, 241 plates in all. 241pp. 9 x 12. 0-486-23004-X

DRAWING DRAPERY FROM HEAD TO TOE, Cliff Young. Expert guidance on how to draw shirts, pants, skirts, gloves, hats, and coats on the human figure, including folds in relation to the body, pull and crush, action folds, creases, more. Over 200 drawings. 48pp. 8¼ x 11. 0-486-45591-2

DUBLINERS, James Joyce. A fine and accessible introduction to the work of one of the 20th century's most influential writers, this collection features 15 tales, including a masterpiece of the short-story genre, "The Dead." 160pp. 5³⁄₁₆ x 8¼. 0-486-26870-5

EASY-TO-MAKE POP-UPS, Joan Irvine. Illustrated by Barbara Reid. Dozens of wonderful ideas for three-dimensional paper fun — from holiday greeting cards with moving parts to a pop-up menagerie. Easy-to-follow, illustrated instructions for more than 30 projects. 299 black-and-white illustrations. 96pp. 8⅜ x 11. 0-486-44622-0

EASY-TO-MAKE STORYBOOK DOLLS: A "Novel" Approach to Cloth Dollmaking, Sherralyn St. Clair. Favorite fictional characters come alive in this unique beginner's dollmaking guide. Includes patterns for Pollyanna, Dorothy from *The Wonderful Wizard of Oz,* Mary of *The Secret Garden,* plus easy-to-follow instructions, 263 black-and-white illustrations, and an 8-page color insert. 112pp. 8¼ x 11. 0-486-47360-0

EINSTEIN'S ESSAYS IN SCIENCE, Albert Einstein. Speeches and essays in accessible, everyday language profile influential physicists such as Niels Bohr and Isaac Newton. They also explore areas of physics to which the author made major contributions. 128pp. 5 x 8. 0-486-47011-3

EL DORADO: Further Adventures of the Scarlet Pimpernel, Baroness Orczy. A popular sequel to *The Scarlet Pimpernel,* this suspenseful story recounts the Pimpernel's attempts to rescue the Dauphin from imprisonment during the French Revolution. An irresistible blend of intrigue, period detail, and vibrant characterizations. 352pp. 5³⁄₁₆ x 8¼. 0-486-44026-5

ELEGANT SMALL HOMES OF THE TWENTIES: 99 Designs from a Competition, Chicago Tribune. Nearly 100 designs for five- and six-room houses feature New England and Southern colonials, Normandy cottages, stately Italianate dwellings, and other fascinating snapshots of American domestic architecture of the 1920s. 112pp. 9 x 12. 0-486-46910-7

THE ELEMENTS OF STYLE: The Original Edition, William Strunk, Jr. This is the book that generations of writers have relied upon for timeless advice on grammar, diction, syntax, and other essentials. In concise terms, it identifies the principal requirements of proper style and common errors. 64pp. 5⅜ x 8½. 0-486-44798-7

THE ELUSIVE PIMPERNEL, Baroness Orczy. Robespierre's revolutionaries find their wicked schemes thwarted by the heroic Pimpernel — Sir Percival Blakeney. In this thrilling sequel, Chauvelin devises a plot to eliminate the Pimpernel and his wife. 272pp. 5³⁄₁₆ x 8¼. 0-486-45464-9

Browse over 9,000 books at www.doverpublications.com